BLOCKCHAIN

Bitcoin, Ethereum, and Cryptocurrency

The Insider's Guide to Blockchain Technology, Bitcoin Mining, Investing and Trading Cryptocurrencies

TABLE OF CONTENTS

CRYPTOCURRENCY

Conclusion

BLOCKCHAIN

Introduction

Conclusion

BITCOIN

Introduction

Conclusion

About the author

CRYPTOCURRENCY

The Ultimate Guide to The World of Cryptocurrency and How I Became a Crypto Millionaire in 6 Months

Chapter 1

INTRODUCING CRYPTOCURRENCY

Chances are if you're reading this book, you've already heard something about Cryptocurrency, and it has definitely peaked your interest. You're probably thinking you'd like to get in the profits that are beckoning you but don't know where to start. Well, you've come to the right place.

Many people believe that cryptocurrency will eventually replace our current economic system. That's a pretty bold statement considering that the system we are using now has been in place for hundreds of years. However, if you've learned anything about economic history, no matter where you came from, whose culture you adopt, or your status in life, the economic and political fabric of the world is never completely set. It is always in a state of flux, and when the systems in place no longer meet the needs of the public, they must change. We are on the precipice of change right now with cryptocurrency.

Ask one hundred people if they know what cryptocurrency is, and you'll probably find that only half of them have ever heard of it, likely half of them have no idea what it is, and the odds are that half of those who do know what it is, have any detailed knowledge. And likely only a small percentage of them actually have earned or invested any money in it.

So, how is it that people are touting this as the next big thing in economic evolution? The answer is simple. While the percentage of people with knowledge of it is still small, the news of this amazing innovative opportunity in economic evolution is spreading. It's spreading because cryptocurrency has already proven to be the perfect solution for many who are already struggling in this harsh and slanted economic environment. The opportunities are endless, and all it takes is a little know-how, and you can start building your new financial portfolio with cryptocurrency and turn a tidy profit in the process.

What Is Cryptocurrency?

Every society since mankind began trading things of value had some type of currency. Notice I used the word currency, not money. The reason for this is because money is merely one form of currency; it is used to transfer VALUE from one party to the next. Now that we are in the digital age, cryptocurrency is simply currency in digital form.

In the past, people used all sorts of things to transfer value from one person to the next. At one point, they were using livestock (cattle, goats, sheep, pigs, chickens, etc.). Later, when carrying around a few cows every time you needed to go shopping turned out to be cumbersome, they began trading shells (conch, puka, conch, etc.) or beads, after that it was bone, metal, and now paper (actually paper money is not really paper at all, it's a secret blend of bamboo and cotton fibers, woven together with silk threads).

But I'm sure you've noticed over the past few years, that the need to carry around physical money is not as important or necessary as it once was. People now do much of their buying and selling either online or with credit or debit cards. Eventually, physical money may completely fade from use. What's now taking its place is cryptocurrency, the next step up in a digital form of currency that is traded and managed entirely online.

The word cryptocurrency itself is a blend of two Greek words, "crypto," which means "to be hidden or to be kept private." In English, we use these as root words quite often. A crypt is a place where you can hide dead bodies, cryptic – to have a mysterious or hidden meaning, cryptography – the study of breaking codes to find their hidden meaning or the practice of solving them.

This is the general idea behind cryptocurrency, the art of writing code (encrypt) or decoding (decrypt). The second word in the blend "currency" refers to the object used to transfer value from one party to the next. Today, that object is money, but in the modern world of cryptocurrency, it is digital code.

It is basically the use of a complex code to encrypt data transfers to exchange value. This is done by creating complex mathematical formulas and unique protocols designed to make the codes virtually impossible to break, counterfeit, or duplicate. These protocols then not only protect the transaction between two parties but they also conceal the identity of all those involved.

The beauty of cryptocurrency is that it is not under the control of any governmental agency, so there is no centralized institution or political entity responsible for determining its value. The value, therefore, is determined primarily by its users and is based on supply and demand. This causes the price to fluctuate more like that of stocks and bonds.

It is used just like you would use a physical currency; you can make purchases, save it, trade it, or even invest it in the same manner. The difference is that you would never hold them in your hands; they only exist as lines of code maintained in a database, and just like with physical currency, you cannot change its value. If you have $20 bill in your hand, there is no way you can change that to $100 or any other value. It is what it is. However, you can always add to it, subtract from it, or save it anytime you like.

History of Cryptocurrency

Cryptocurrency, like all other innovations, was created to solve a particular problem. In the beginning, it was never meant to become the preferred currency of trade but was to be used as a side product to complement an already existing digital currency system. You probably had no idea that each time you used your debit card, credit card, or had an automatic deposit sent to your bank account, you were using digital currency. Each time you paid your bills online, you were using digital currency. While these tools certainly made life simpler, they presented a major problem, that of double spending. Double spending simply meant that the same money could be spent twice, simply because it could easily be copied. There was always a risk that the possessor could replicate the currency and send it to another party and still hold on to the original.

However, with the introduction of cryptocurrency, for the first time, people could use digital currency without going through a centralized server, without any specialized regulation, or a single authority overseeing everything. The system was based entirely on P2P (person to person) networks used as an assurance against double spending.

While it may not have been the original intent of this new monetary instrument, another issue that cryptocurrency resolved was creating a system that eliminated the need for a third-party to be involved in transactions. This automatically provided a more secure system for making online payments. It also eliminated the cost of having to pay exorbitant fees for every transaction made. The new digital currency was designed to be completely independent of any type of central regulation or third-party involvement.

Actually, the original intent for cryptocurrency was as a wealth enrichment tool. As there is a cap on the amount of cryptocurrency available on the market, the more people use it, the higher the demand. Therefore, over time, the value of the currency will gradually increase.

With this system, all transactions take place between the two parties involved and no any other third parties. No transaction takes place unless there is an absolute consensus and no funds can be transferred unless it is legitimate.

What Makes Cryptocurrency Different from Normal Currency?

There is not much difference between cryptocurrency and our traditional currency when it comes to spending. You can use them to purchase anything you can purchase with regular currency as long as the other party is willing to trade with them.

With more than 1000 cryptocurrencies available to choose from and more coming there's a pretty good bet that no matter what type of business you want to conduct you will be able to trade using some form of cryptocurrency. The biggest and probably the most well-known among them is the Bitcoin, but we'll talk more about that in the next Chapter.

Quite often, you will hear them referred to as coins: Bitcoin, Dogecoin, Litecoin, etc. but the word is used only as a point of reference. Cryptocurrency does not have a physical form. Still, there are some similarities, but the differences make them unique.

They are same that they can assign value and are just as liquid as any other type of currency with the exception that they use encryption and decryption techniques to document every transaction.

The cryptography not only keeps the details of the transaction secure but also protects the identity of the parties involved as well.

Chapter 2

THE MOST COMMON CRYPTOCURREN-CIES

As more and more places of business are in a position to accept a digital currency as payment for their product or services, cryptocurrencies will gradually begin to overtake physical money. But unless you're dealing with them on a regular basis, you're probably not aware of how many different cryptocurrencies are already floating around the market.

One of the unique advantages of cryptocurrency is that they are created to fulfill a void in the economy. Unlike traditional dollars and coins, a cryptocurrency can be designed to achieve a certain purpose. Of course, not all cryptocurrencies are the same. Because they are so easy to create, some have been developed as a joke, others for scams, and still others for special events or occasions.

However, there are plenty of solid digital currencies to choose from so depending on your needs; there is no doubt that you will find the perfect one for you.

Below we will take a closer look at some of the most common currencies available and see why they are so important.

1. Bitcoin

Most likely when you think of digital currency, Bitcoin is the name that comes to your mind. Just like the name Xerox is almost synonymous with copy, Bitcoin is often confused and believed to be the only cryptocurrency around. Some people actually refer to it as the "people's currency" because they expect it to be the one cryptocurrency that will uproot and replace all national currencies in the future.

Bitcoin was created by a mysteriously anonymous figure, Satoshi Nakamoto, it was the very first digital currency of its kind. It holds the largest market cap to date, placing it well over any other currency on the list.

For those interested in investing in cryptocurrencies, the best place to start is with Bitcoin. It is without a doubt the leader of the pack and has had the longest history of any other coins on the market. As a matter of fact, all other coins are referred to as altcoins (alternative coins) because they are viewed as alternatives to Bitcoin.

People use them to buy or sell and even to pay for services both on and offline. It is even possible now to pick up Bitcoins through ATM being introduced in some different countries.

While it does require the use of codes to buy or sell Bitcoins, it is not necessary to understand all the technical details to get the benefits they offer.

2. Ethereum (Ether)

Like Bitcoin, Ethereum is a public Blockchain digital currency with a few technical differences. Where Bitcoin is geared more towards keeping track of who owns the currency, Ethereum is designed more towards the function of the programming code.

Ethereum is most known for its use of Smart Contracts, offering people the ability to code and enact very definite contract terms without the involvement of a third-party. At its basic level, it solves the problem of handling legal contracts online. When a smart contract is put into motion, it works like a self-operating computer program designed to take action automatically once agreed upon conditions are met. Whatever the system is programmed to do, it will follow those procedures exactly. There is no possibility to censor or interfere with the parameters set.

Another unique feature of Ethereum is that there are very few limitations on Ethereum's ability to process code. A developer is free to come up with thousands of different applications, so its potential is virtually endless.

This currency has been divided into two distinct forms: Ethereum (ETH) and Ethereum

Classic (ETC). Created in 2015 by Vitalik Buterin, it has already reached a market cap of more than $1 billion.

3. Ripple

Not only is Ripple a digital currency but it is also an open payment network where users can transfer currency from one party to the next. It is designed to work pretty much the same way that Bitcoin does on a decentralized network using the same format that the Internet does with the information.

Its purpose is to make a connection between different payment systems used by different parties. It eliminates the snags of different companies using different systems, so that transfer of funds is practically seamless regardless of the country it is going to.

Not only it will give users the ability to connect with users of other forms of digital currency, but it will also speed up the transfer process and provide more stability. With Ripple, there is no need to wait for confirmation, so every transaction goes through quickly.

4. Monero

One of the biggest problems people deal within online technology is that of maintaining privacy, which is Monero's primary concern. While this may present a problem in most western governments, Monero is extremely important in nations where one's identity must be protected at all costs. For example, in the USA when people are concerned about their identity, it is about protecting their assets. They don't want someone to come in and steal the value they have accumulated. However, for someone who lives in places where playing on the economic playground could be perceived as anti-government, secrecy could mean your life.

In addition to being private, it is secure, and anything traded through Monero is untraceable. It uses its own unique cryptography that ensures that every transaction made cannot be linked to the parties involved. This is accomplished through the use of multiple keys. Unlike other cryptocurrencies where the user may have one public view key and one private view key, with Monero your public key is provided to generate a one-time public address. The private key, however, is given to the receiver to scan the Blockchain to search for the funds they are to receive.

But you will also have a public spend key, a private spend key, which has their own unique functions they are to perform.

One of the reasons Monero is so popular is because you can maintain total control over all of your transactions. Therefore, you and only you are responsible for what happens to your money. It is also fungible meaning, and no one can know the history of the money you received.

5. Litecoin

Litecoin is very similar to Bitcoin when it comes to code, but there are a few significant functional differences.

While both currencies have the same purpose, Litecoin processes much faster than Bitcoin. Since Bitcoin transactions are not complete until they have received confirmation, users must "wait" for "miners" to verify every transaction. This process could take as little as 10 minutes, but it could also take much longer. Litecoin does the same thing in an even shorter time frame.

Like Bitcoin, it is a peer-to-peer currency that provides immediate payments to anyplace in the world for a minuscule fee. The same powerful mathematical equations used to provide the network's security also gives each user the ability to manage their own finances.

Litecoin uses what is called an Open Source Protocol, which lets developers know where to access the user's source code.

6. Golem

The Golem Network has been compared to the Airbnb for computers allowing its users to rent out their computing power to other users online. It allows other machines located in different places around the globe to transact and work together on a particular project.

Golem also takes advantage of the same smart contracts capabilities that Ethereum uses. However, like Ethereum allows the user to buy fuel, cars, and pay their owners, Golem does the same thing with computer power.

Through Golem users help to create the world's largest supercomputer, an interplanetary network comprised of everything from personal laptops in people's homes to entire data centers; all completely decentralized, meaning no one is monitoring its works.

This network would not be owned, managed, or operated by any individual, government, or corporation and it cannot be utilized to monopolize the economy or regulate people's abilities to control their own money, and it can never be shut down.

When your computer joins the Golem system it could be used to perform scientific research, render graphics, create Artificial Intelligence, analyze data, or mine for a cryptocurrency.

7. Factom

One of the things that Factom is known for is its ability to solve many business challenges because of how it maintains unalterable records.

It creates a layer of data using the Bitcoin Blockchain as its foundation. Their distributed ledger technology can maintain millions of records on a Blockchain with just one hash.

Businesses, as well as governments, can both use Factom as a means of documenting their data in a way that prevents it from being altered, deleted, or backdated in any way. This assures that all data stored remains intact and ensures user privacy at the same time.

Because this information is stored on a decentralized network, the threat of hackers or organizations and their attempts to tamper or interfere with its processes is virtually impossible.

Through Factom, users can store all kinds of data making it perfect for all sorts of applications. Medical records, supply chain management, legal applications, and more can make use of this type of cryptocurrency.

As we said before, there are now more than a thousand cryptocurrencies to choose from, and more are being created regularly. When it comes to investing or doing business with these currencies, it's important that you learn as much as you can about each one.

It can be really exciting to think about the potential each of these has, but you must proceed with caution. While there are much available, you need to know that the currency you choose has the opportunity to bring you the results you seek. This requires that you ask the right questions.

It is not enough that the currency you choose can be used to purchase or sell a product. If you want to make money using cryptocurrency, it also has to be appealing to the masses. Remember, the value of any currency is not backed up by any government or organization but is determined by the basics of supply and demand. For that to happen, it must solve a particular problem.

You'll notice that all the currencies listed above address a unique problem. However, some digital currencies solve problems but not those problems that many people must deal with.

It means that only a few will see a need to trade with those currencies thus limiting your profit potential.

Whatever problem these currencies address, it must be something you understand. Take the time to learn about the technology behind it, learn about its developers and the team who put it together. It can also be beneficial if you can visualize where that currency will go in the future and see yourself as part of its ultimate goal.

Also, it is important to know which merchants you might expect to accept that currency and decide if you are likely to be dealing with that type of business.

Once you've learned and understood all of these things, your first decision investing in cryptocurrency is made. You are ready for the next step.

Chapter 3

HOW I BECAME A CRYPTOCURRENCY MILLIONAIRE IN 6 MONTHS

"So my view's quite clear. I believe cryptocurrencies, bitcoin is the first example; I believe they're going to change the world." – **Richard Brown, Executive Architect at IBM**

Being a millionaire isn't quite as unique as it used to be. In 2015, there were 10.1 million American households—that's 8.3 percent of the total population—with a net worth of at least $1 million, compared to just 5.9 percent in the heart of the Great Recession.

Yet, hitting the million-dollar mark remains a landmark goal for Americans. For many, it symbolizes ultimate financial freedom.

While it's easy to assume that people with millions in the bank got there by inheriting family money or raking in massive salaries, plenty earn their fortunes by living frugally, investing wisely and creating their own income-producing opportunities.

My story started in 2012, I was a college student, and later that year, I read and started talking about how I thought the world would switch to Bitcoin like any second now. In 2009, I thought the USD was ready to collapse (and put my money in gold). I was recently out of the military and spent time into self-reliance stuff with my brother; we had a multi-acre "compound/mini-farm" with as many as 10 people living there.

I'm sharing this to explain that I was just lucky to be reading about this kind of stuff and alt-currencies at that specific time. Anyway, I tried and gave up buying bitcoin a few times, but I started buying in earnest soon after Coinbase showed up.

So, how can you make insane money with cryptocurrencies?

One word: Altcoins.

Altcoins stand for 'alternative coins,' or in simple terms, the cryptocurrency that's NOT Bitcoin.

There's Bitcoin, and then there's 'everything else.'

'Everything else' is what altcoins are.

Invest in altcoins, the right ones, and you can make insane amounts of money and fast.

ALTCOINS: The New Way to Earn Big

Now everyone probably has heard of Bitcoin and how much value Bitcoin seems to be gain-ing (it's gone over 3x value in just a year and thousands of times since the start of it in 2008).

It's painful to hear about how much Bitcoin has increased in value since 2008.

I too wanted to buy a bunch of bitcoins back in 2013 when Bitcoin crashed down to about $60.

There are plenty of stories told online about people buying thousands of Bitcoins for $10's apiece years ago, then cashing out when Bitcoin hit $50.

Now you could invest only in Bitcoin right now and just sit on your Bitcoin for a few years.

I feel that Bitcoin may indeed hit $10,000, $20,000, $30,000 and more over the next few years. Some analysts have even said Bitcoin could reach $100,000 in ten years. But this may be a few years away. Despite dips over the years, the Bitcoin trend has only been going up.

However, if you invest in Bitcoin, you may see double or triple over the next few years. But you won't see the returns you would have had if you bought Bitcoin back in 2013 when it was $60.

With Bitcoin roaring towards $5000 a coin now, you can't help but feel the train has already left.

However, if you feel you've missed the real gains with Bitcoin, you haven't.

There's plenty of other opportunities out there if you look at Altcoins.

If you pick the right Altcoin, you can see huge returns.

2x,3x,5x,10x,30x,100x and more.

If you buy Bitcoin right now for $4000 and wait a year for Bitcoin to reach $8000, you've made 2X (200 percent).

But there's plenty of altcoins you can buy now and hold for just a few weeks (or months) and see 2X, 5X, 10X, even 100X return!

Now, it's not necessarily easy to get these huge returns. It takes an investment on your part, a leap of faith and a hell of a lot of research to pick the RIGHT coin that has that chance.

Many altcoins are under 1 dollar (even a couple cents or less). It's these cheaper coins that have a chance to explode.

You have the opportunity to get cheaper coins that could explode in value over time (and some have).

I can personally verify this because I've made some huge returns in some of my investments. I've chosen some coins that have gone 4X (400 percent) in just a month. Several that did 6X (600%) to 8X (800 percent)

You might think that making these ridiculous gains is pie-in-the-sky, but it happens more often than you might think.

One of the best recent examples is Ethereum, the second most valuable cryptocurrency. Ethereum is only a couple years old, but in one year it has exploded from $10 to over 300 dollars (its all-time high was 400+ dollars).

I've talked about the general strategy for how to make money with cryptocurrency.

Now, let's talk about what I did, which was the point of this chapter!

The only two coins I hold currently are Bitcoin and Ethereum. Most of my gains came from Ethereum.

I was lucky (smart?) enough to buy the vast majority of my ETH below $13. My logic was twofold:

1. Until Bitcoin resolves its scaling issues, it's a sure-fire bet that other currencies will take the lead over time. The longer Bitcoin scaling remains unresolved, the more other currencies will grow.

2. The best choice to me appeared to be Ethereum, based on its development

roadmap. I have learned (mostly from reading articles) to invest in something with utility and value. To me, Ethereum is such a coin. Bitcoin only has first-mover advantage left, and Core devs are presently destroying that.

I used the above knowledge to my advantage when investing. And it paid off. Also, it's worth noting that even if Bitcoin Scaling does get resolved, the resolution process itself (forking) will likely be a messy bloodbath. I consider this another invaluable piece of investing knowledge. I invite you to use it.

You don't always have certainties in investing, but I feel point #1 above, and Bitcoin's scaling-resolution-bloodbath are two certainties you can use to your advantage.

I think Bitcoin will eventually recover, but not after a forceful removal of the current devs. This may be at their own hands by forking themselves off the main network via a very foolish UASF.

I hope many of you are achieving similar success in your investing.

Coin Cap (for iOS) is the app I use to track my money. I recommend it for an easy way to track your crypto holdings. You can fingerprint lock it too, which I find nice for security.

I'd like to thank everybody in my group and my brother for your insightful posts and friendly correspondence. Let's keep it that way (not like the Bitcoin space which is highly toxic right now and very unpleasant).

And around June 18th, I too joined the ranks of the crypto wealthy, or crypto millionaires. Granted I'm not really a 'whale' as the term goes just yet, with only about 1 million dollars right now in crypto coins — there are guys out there with hundreds of millions playing with crypto, even billions.

ALTFOLIO

$1,043,954.58

+6.78% today

| Today | 1W | 1M | 3M | 6M | 1Y | ALL |

| **Main Crypto** | Altfolio 2 | Altfolio 3 |

🔍 Search Coins   Price by Market Cap ▾

Ⓑ Bitcoin BTC $2,006.81
   💰 65.61368 BTC $131,674.19

◆ Ethereum ETH $138.04
   💰 6,608.649 ETH $912,280.39

Add A Coin   ⊕

Now, my portfolio is small, and I only touched
1 million US dollars in crypto wealth (there are
some people with vast sums), but I'm on the
first step to a greater journey.

Chapter 4

HOW DOES CRYPTOCURRENCY WORK?

Just like with any traditional currency, you can use cryptocurrency to make purchases both in the store and online. You can also use them as investment tools or as a means of trading or bartering. While digital currency doesn't necessarily have a face value as in a physical instrument, you can hold it in your hand and carry it from one place to the next via your "wallet." In essence, your wallet holds the lines of code that connects you to your currency maintained in the database. Once all the conditions of a transaction are met, the currency can be transferred to the individual or organization for completion.

While this explanation may sound a little complicated, there is really very little difference between conducting a transaction in a traditional bank and trading in cryptocurrency. When you put your money into a bank account, there are certain conditions that you must meet to reclaim it. You may be asked to provide identification, a history of past transactions, or give a signature that matches one they have on file.

In this case, the bank serves as the third-party to verify the data they have on file before you can make any changes to your account. With cryptocurrency, however, you eliminate the middleman, and through the use of a code, you are the party responsible for ensuring that all the conditions are met before deciding to transfer the funds.

There are several steps involved in making a cryptocurrency transaction.

1. The transaction is submitted online

2. The request is received by the P2P network nodes.

3. The network then verifies the identity of the requester and the details of the transaction.

4. The miners then verify, accept, or deny the request

5. If approved, it is logged into the digital database (the Blockchain)

6. The transaction is then added to a list of stored lines of code. (Once entered here, it can never be altered or deleted.

7. The transaction is then listed as complete.

While there are quite a few steps involved in this type of transaction, it can usually be finalized in just a matter of minutes.

The system is quite efficient and very easy to do. Still, let's take a look at what happens in just a little more detail.

Encryption/Decryption

Encryption is simply the tool used to convert the data relating to the transaction into a line of code. This is done to keep all but the interested parties from accessing the information. Just as you have passwords and key codes to get information on your bank account online, your digital currency will do the same but in a little more detail. The user will create two keys that are linked to each other by a mathematical equation. The public key is used to create the code, which is called the encryption and the second key, called the private key is used to decode or decrypt the code.

When you are ready to make a payment or purchase, you can do so by giving the other party the public key, which gives them access to your virtual wallet. However, for them to collect on your payment, they must also have the private key, which gives them access to the allocated funds.

8. Decentralized

Cryptocurrency removes the decision-making power from a central location and transfers it to the parties involved. Rather than having all the data maintained on a single server, the information is stored on a network of centric systems that all follow the same basic mathematical rules that have already been agreed upon.

With a decentralized network, no individual or group has a lot of control over what happens to the money. Its value is determined by the people who are actually using the system. Since every person is connected to every other person, there is no centralized point of weakness where it can fail and impact a mass number of members.

Distributed Systems

Closely related to the decentralized network, a distributed system is a network of autonomous computers that are joined together with middleware. They all share the same resources and perform similar functions for users within an integrated network.

These collections of computers work together as one single unit and share the processing power provided by millions of personal computers around the globe. Those who wish to become a part of this type of network generally must first download and run a small program that kicks on whenever the computer is out of use.

Open Source Code

An open source code is a software program that anyone can inspect, modify, and enhance. It usually comes with a license allowing programmers to adjust the software in a way that may support their needs. To open source code, the software must meet several different criteria:

- Free redistribution of software

Allows the user to sell or give away the software as a part of an aggregate distribution program from other sources. As a condition of the license, they cannot demand a royalty or fee for this distribution.

- Availability of source code

The source code must be made available and distribution must be allowed along with the compiled form. How to obtain the source code must be well publicized and made available through the Internet for a reasonable cost.

- Derived works

Licenses must permit the code to be modified and the works resulting from the modifications must be free to be distributed under the same conditions as the license associated with the original software.

- Integrity of the author's source code

Restrictions on modifying the source code are only allowed if the license permits "patch files" to be distributed when the intent is to modify the program during a build time. It must be clearly stated in the license that the distribution can only come from a modified source code and may require derived works to use a different name from the original software.

- Anti-discrimination policies

Distribution of an open source code cannot discriminate in any way against any person or group.

- No discrimination against any specific field or endeavor

There can also be no discrimination against any type of business or any particular endeavor. Distribution cannot be refused by any group or organization.

- Distribution of License

Rights to the program apply to any group or organization it is distributed to.

- License cannot be limited to any specific product

It cannot be dependent on any program or any specific distribution.

- It cannot be allowed to restrict any other software program.

It is not permitted to require any other program to also be open-source or come in any other form.

- It must be technology-neutral

It cannot rely on any individual technology or interface.

With open source code, there are different types of licenses that allow for programmers to modify their software under certain conditions.

There are several advantages of using open source code

1. You get a higher quality of results when the source code is continuously being modified. Each time it is passed around it is tested and modified, improving the code with each phase.

2. It is a great way for programmers to learn and apply new skills to many popular programs.

3. Many believe the open source code is more reliable and secure than the proprietary software as problems are more likely to be identified and corrected.

4. It is more likely to be available for longer since it is found in the public domain.

5. In most cases, it is free to use and modify,

Public Ledgers (Blockchain)

At the very heart of the database is the public ledger. Sometimes referred to as the Blockchain, it is a public recording of every transaction made on the network.

The public ledger maintains a continuous list of "blocks" where each transaction is recorded in linear and chronological order. As each block is added the ledger, each computer connected to the network (node) automatically receives a downloaded copy.

Transaction

A transaction is created when you use an encrypted electronic signature to send any type of digital currency. It is then added to the Blockchain via a public ledger that is sent out to every node in the network.

Node

Any computer that is part of the global network and is using the protocol to allow the nodes to communicate with each other is a node. Each node is able to authenticate or verify every transaction in the block.

It takes the data from the transaction and verifies every detail and then reconciles it against
its own ledger to ensure that the funds have
not already been spent. If it receives any information that is incorrect, it will first reject
the transaction and will cease all communication with you. This forces the node with incorrect information to be isolated and forced out
of the system.

Mining

The process of verifying transactions and adding them to the Blockchain or the public ledger
is called mining. This involves collecting all
transactions and forming them into blocks and
solving the mathematical codes. It's sort of a
first come first served basis. Any computer
that solves the puzzle first gets to add the next
block to the Blockchain and gets a reward for
finding the solution.

Since every transaction takes place with an
entire network of peers, everyone in the system has the same access to all transaction his-
tories. Even if a database cannot be changed,
everyone will still have access to every transaction in the entire network including the identities of each participant (encoded). Each record
will also contain the buyer or seller's private
keys, which contain all the confirmations of
each transaction.

When a new transaction is established, it is automatically entered into the system, and once all the confirmation processes are verified, every single peer on the network will receive it.

If no confirmation is done, the request never moves beyond the initial stage and can be canceled. However, once they have been confirmed, it is added to the Blockchain; from then on, it is impossible to alter. The miner's job is to confirm all those transactions within the network.

Anyone with the right hardware can enter the system as a peer and become a miner.

Chapter 5

INVESTMENT

There are many ways you can make money using cryptocurrency. These digital currencies are becoming more and more popular with time, and the options for profit are many. Depending on your preference you can choose to buy or sell them, become a miner, or offer a product or service for them over dedicated platforms.

Whatever you choose to do there are several applications that can be used to help you first find the type of cryptocurrency you want to invest in and make your investment. But before you even think about that you must take some time to learn how to convert your traditional money into a digital currency.

Cryptocurrency Exchange Platform

Just like when exchanging traditional currency, digital currencies have exchange houses where they can be traded. These exchange houses usually work in a similar way to a financial institution where you can save your money, trade, offer or receive loans.

These exchange houses are important as they will usually be the first and last stop whenever you're dealing with cryptocurrencies. Keep in mind that these exchange houses are not limited to only one type of currency but can offer several different ones. This is very helpful because you could buy and trade in one currency and then switch to another currency whenever you feel like it.

As these exchange houses play such an important role in your investment strategy, it is necessary to make sure you choose one carefully. This decision isn't just a matter of finding the house with the best transaction fees or how many different types of payments they accept, but you must also investigate the different types of cryptocurrencies they offer and find those that are most likely to match up with your investment goals.

When choosing digital currencies, the most commonly traded is the Bitcoin so as a beginning investor, it is probably smart to start with a proven success. It is easy to find an exchange house that will accommodate them as opposed to those that are less popular. It may take you a while to find a house that can accommodate those less recognized in the cryptocurrency world.

Not only are Bitcoins commonly traded for many types of traditional currency but they can be traded for other digital currencies as well. So, as you're investigating exchange houses, it will be helpful to understand the different trading pairs that each house is offering, so you know your options.

When it comes to service fees, while they may not be the most important factor in choosing an exchange house, they are definitely worth considering. Depending on the exchange house you choose, you could find yourself paying a fraction of a percentage for each transaction to as much as 5% of your total earnings. However, there are also additional fees you need to factor into your choice of exchange houses. Many exchange houses will require a monthly service fee for housing your digital currency while others may demand an additional deposit or withdrawal fee. These are fees that are most likely to get you into trouble when investing in cryptocurrency, so the more you familiarize yourself with these, the less likely you'll see your profits eaten away by these additional charges before you ever get to see any of it.

Always keep in mind that exchanges are not regulated like government-backed financial institutions. So, there is very little you can do if one of them folds and your money disappears. It is important that you do your due diligence and make sure of everything before you invest your money. Look for exchange houses that have a long-standing reputation and evaluate their security protocols before making any decisions. If you find a house with very little information about their track record, consider it as a warning that they may not have been around for very long and have no proof of staying power. It is better to take heed and move on.

The Cryptocurrency Wallet

No matter which cryptocurrency you want to invest in or which exchange house you use, you will have to set up a digital wallet. Many exchange houses offer you a wallet as part of their service, but others may require you to set up your own wallet by a third-party for storing your currency.

If you choose to go through a third-party storage facility, there are some good ones available to choose from. Wallets usually have a fixed rate that applies whether you're buying or selling. All you have to do is link your bank card or your bank account information to your wallet, and you're set up to make transactions.

There are pros and cons to investing in cryptocurrency in this way. First, on the positive side, you can make transactions very quickly and easily through the wallet. You can liken it to making an online purchase with your credit or debit card, enter the necessary details, verify your identity and you're done. You can even make these types of purchases through special ATMs that now offer cryptocurrencies.

If you're more concerned about time, then this is one of the best ways to go.

However, you will also find that not all transaction pairs are offered this way. In many cases, getting your cryptocurrency exchanged for traditional funds may not always be easy. But a bigger issue to be concerned with is your risk of exposing your personal information and payment data. One of the reasons people choose to trade in cryptocurrency is because they want the anonymity that is offered in dealing with every transaction.

Peer-to-Peer

Another way to obtain cryptocurrency is to buy it from your peers. If you know someone who owns the kind of currency you want, you can simply buy directly from them. In fact, there are exchange houses that are set up simply to connect private buyers and sellers to each other. You can also find someone to trade with through online community forums.

If you don't have a personal network of traders set up, you can check with your wallet provider or online for local and private trading tools already built into the system. With these tools, you can find sellers living right in your immediate area that you can meet with and negotiate a trade.

It is important however if you choose to go this route then you verify the seller's reputation through testimonials, online checks, or whatever means necessary to verify that they are legitimate. Remember, there is little recourse if you are taken in a scam, so make sure you find someone you can trust before you agree to anything.

Finally, if you choose to buy and sell privately, make sure that you conduct your business in a public arena. It should go without saying that meeting strangers for the first time to do a monetary transaction does not come without risk. Being in a public place with lots of people around can be more of a protection than you might realize.

Credit Card

In today's world, you can use credit cards to buy just about anything, including cryptocurrency. There are loads of online payment systems that will allow you to buy cryptocurrency using on credit.

Still, while this method is very easy, caution is still warranted. As a matter of fact, until you have a solid, long-lasting, established relationship with anyone, it is always best to err on the side of caution to make sure that everything they do and every interaction you have with them is completely above board.

Most of these platforms will accept Visa and MasterCard, but there are others that are capable of accepting other credit cards as well.

Wire Purchase

You can also purchase via wire. There are some exchanges or private individuals that will accept a wire transfer as a form of payment. However, this is probably the less popular choice as these transactions can literally take days to complete.

Online Payment Systems

Purchasing cryptocurrency using alternative payment systems like PayPal or some other form of online payment can be just as easy as purchasing using your bank or credit card. With the option, it is easy to set up an account with just your email address then link your card or bank account to the system. Once done, you can complete a transaction quickly and easily.

The only drawback to this system is the additional service fees in place. However, these fees can actually be viewed as a protection as they almost always come with some sort of protocol in place to handle dispute resolution when things don't necessarily go as planned.

Buy with Cash

This is especially beneficial when you're purchasing your digital currency from a peer. You can pay with cash when you meet or use cash transferred from your digital wallet at the point of agreement. This is probably the fastest mode of payment when buying cryptocurrency of all.

As you can see, there are many options when it comes to taking the first step in investing in cryptocurrency. While all of these options are good, there is no system without its flaws. Make sure you do your homework and get background on anyone that you plan to do business with. In the beginning, you may be unsure of which avenue will work best for you, so you might want to try several different tools to make sure you find the one that will work best for you.

Before You Invest

Now that you know all of your options for buying you need to make sure you do everything in the right order. This will help you to avoid having to pay any additional fees or getting bogged down in unnecessary steps to get started. Most of these guidelines listed below are just plain common sense but investing in digital currency can be exciting and when we get too excited about something we forget to dot the i's and cross the t's.

1. **Determine your budget:** Investing in anything requires a starting capital, so do a little price shopping. Once you know how much money you can afford to invest, it will be easy to determine which currencies you can buy.

2. **Determine the currency:** Next you want to decide which currency you want to buy. With so much available it is best to start with the most commonly traded on the market. There are lots of online resources that can give you some background knowledge about each type of coin, its history, and its potential for future placement on the market.

3. **Choose your exchange:** Once you know the currency then begin by choosing which exchange you want to trade in. This will be the platform from where you will start every transaction. While many exchanges offer a variety of digital currencies, they may not all have the same menu or the same prices. Research them thoroughly before you set up an account. Don't forget to investigate their fee schedule and their payment methods as well.

4. **Set up your wallet:** If the exchange house you select comes with your own wallet you can skip this step, but if you have to go outside to set up your wallet with a third-party then you will have to investigate further. It is important to understand that not all wallets are created equal. You will find several different types of wallets, and you may discover that you need more than one.

Insurance

It is always best to earn on the side of caution and insurance is one of the best ways to do that. There are some exchange houses that offer insurance coverage to protect your currency, or you can choose to work with third-party carriers but be warned these may come at an additional cost.

Start Buying

Now it is time to start building up your crypto portfolio. As we discussed before you can begin by buying and selling on the exchange, but you can also connect with other people or websites to purchase your currency. To make your purchase, all you need to do is give them your public key in your wallet so they can transfer the currency to your account.

Trade

Once you have collected enough cryptocurrency, you may decide that you want to trade it for another type of currency. Once all the steps are done, you can easily make a trade through your exchange house or any exchange house that is set up to exchange currencies for your particular pair.

No matter what decisions you make, it is always important to ask a lot of questions before you make a final decision to invest. Remember, you will be dealing with assets that are not physical, so you won't walk away with some-thing in your hand.

It's not like negotiating for a car where at the end of the process you can drive it off the lot. Everything will always remain in the digital realm, so you need to verify everything and then double check it to make sure you're get-ting what you're paying for.

When looking at a currency, you want to find something that will not only give you a good trade now but has the potential for generating earnings in the future. Look for currencies that have the credibility and the history to show that you will be able to hold onto your money.

Make sure that the currency you choose is not going to drop in value overnight. It is normal for a price to fluctuate up and down over time but the currency that makes drastic drops is something to be wary of.

Ask yourself if you plan to be in this for the long haul or are you looking for short-term returns. Once you're set up, it is just as easy to exit a trade as it is to get into it. However, in determining how long you will stay will de-pend on what type of market you want to play in. A bullish market is more favorable to buy-ers, a bearish market is more favorable to sellers, and a break-even market is just what it says it is.

Beginners usually rely on several basic strategies until they get comfortable with the market. They may start with something as simple as arbitrage where transactions are made very quickly. You buy low and sell high. Since there are no standard market rates to go by, you can buy from one market and sell the same day to another market and make a profit as you do.

It's about seeking out and exploiting the opportunities you find. It's an easy way to earn a profit but be wary of the fees, or you may find yourself losing money in the process.

Another strategy that beginners often use is short-term trading. In these cases, investors buy currency as the price is slowly inching up and then hold onto it watching as the price moves beyond what was paid for it. Then they sell it making a tidy little profit along the way. The entire transaction can be done in a matter of hours or days. Doing this on a regular basis could bring in a steady income if you keep your eye out for the right margin.

The Top Cryptocurrencies to Invest in 2017

While the decision on which currency you choose will always lie with you, experts have made several recommendations for the currencies that show the best potential for 2017.

Bitcoin:

As always, Bitcoin is leading the pack as the currency with the most potential. With a market cap at over $75 billion, you can buy one Bitcoin at a little more than $3,600 (as of September 2017). This makes it the most expensive of cryptocurrencies on the market today.

If you're not ready to put that much down on a single Bitcoin, you can start by a Satoshi (the smallest fraction of a Bitcoin). It is the equivalent of 000,000,001 of a full Bitcoin. That means that if you buy 1 Satoshi at $3,641 a single Satoshi can cost you only $0.00004019, which amounts to only a fraction of a cent in USD.

Ethereum

Another great cryptocurrency to start investing in is Ethereum (sometimes referred to as Ether). It is an open-source, public, blockchain-based distributed computing platform featuring smart contract (scripting) functionality. It provides a decentralized Turing-complete virtual machine, the Ethereum Virtual Machine (EVM), which can execute scripts using an international network of public nodes. Today's market cap for Ethereum is nearly $31 million with a price of about $328 for a single coin.

Ethereum has been steadily growing month by month increasing its potential for profit as it does so. It has a proven track record that allows its team of developers to solve issues on a real-time basis.

Monero

Monero is gaining popularity because of its perfect world of anonymity. Because they go to great lengths to keep the identity of the investor private, many people are flocking to it. Unlike with other cryptocurrencies that maintain anonymity, once you give your wallet address to anyone they can see all of the transactions you have made in the past. While they cannot see the identity of who you traded with without decoding the information, it is clear that your secrecy is only as strong as your code.

With Monero, it is different. Its software is designed to mix your coins with other investor's coins, so you have no idea of who owns what or how much.

The market cap for Monero is approximately 1/100th of a Bitcoin, which makes it a much more affordable investment in the long run.

Ripple

Ripple is the name for both a digital currency (XRP) and an open payment network within which the currency is transferred. It is a distributed, open-source payments system that's still in beta. The goal of the ripple system, according to its website, is to enable people to break free of the "walled gardens" of financial networks – i.e., credit cards, banks, PayPal and other institutions that restrict access with fees, charges for currency exchanges and processing delays.

Ripple has become more popular mainly because its software allows transactions to be conducted almost instantaneously. It also drastically reduces the cost of transaction fees making it extremely favorable for the investor.

It is believed that Ripple will exceed the market capitalization of Bitcoin by March 2018 at the latest.

Ripple is simply what Bitcoin didn't manage to become: an efficient tool to transfer value and assets trusted by people and institutions.

Ripple has been accepted by over 70 (and counting) banks, some of them are definitively big names (UBS, BoA, BBVA, NBAD...)

Should You Invest in Cryptocurrency?

Cryptocurrency is a very new and innovative system that is appealing in many ways for an investor. There are several reasons why people are now taking a closer look at investing in cryptocurrency.

1. Security: While there is no such thing as 100% security in dealing with cryptocurrency, these coins are considered to be a much safer investment than housing traditional money.

2. Value: Aside from the security, when any asset you invest in has the potential to see a 30% increase in the value of the course of just a few weeks, it is certainly going to attract the attention of many people.

3. Autonomy: As it is not backed by any government or organization, its autonomy doesn't allow it to be controlled by geographical limitations, financial preferences, or political entities.

4. Decentralized: Finally, the fact that the investments are not held on a centralized server making it much more difficult for hackers to access to it and compromise the system. Its value, therefore, is based more on supply and demand rather than by some third-party management system.

However, there are also very bad reasons to invest in cryptocurrencies. Many people fall victim to the hype surrounding every cryptocurrency-bubble. There is always somebody captured by FOMO (fear of missing out), buying massively in at the peak of a bubble, just in hope to make quick money, while not understanding cryptocurrencies at all. That's a bad reason. Don't do this.

Learn before you invest. It's not just a matter of you should invest, but also a matter of how to invest. Start by educating yourself. Learn about the currency, what affects it, what are its advantages and disadvantages, etc.

My personal advice to you;

Never invest more than you are willing/able to lose – Bitcoin and other cryptocurrencies are a very risky investment, and you should keep that in your mind all the times.

If you want to invest in cryptocurrencies, Bitcoin is still a standard item of every portfolio – but it is no longer the onliest asset. I personally had invested in Bitcoin and Ethereum and luckily I was able to make a fortune with these two. In every well-balanced crypto-portfolio today you find other coins, like:

• Ethereum

• Ripple

• Litecoin

• Dash

• Monero

Chapter 6

MINING

If you've read anything about cryptocurrency, you've heard the term "mining" repeated quite often. While you may have a pretty good idea of what mining is in the physical sense, you may be a little confused about its role in the world of digital currencies.

Now let's get a little deeper into how cryptocurrency transactions are done. A crucial part of this process is what is called mining. While the process happens with all digital currencies, we'll use the Bitcoin as our primary example as we explain this rather complicated process.

What Is Cryptocurrency Mining?

With traditional currency, its value is determined or backed by the government that issued it however with cryptocurrency, there is no governmental backing, so how is the value determined? Essentially, it comes from a complicated series of mathematical computations referred to as "mining." The purpose of these calculations is twofold,

1) it confirms the transactions

2) it keeps the network security intact.

One of the great things about mining crypto-currency is the monetary rewards you can gain. Imagine being able to earn thousands of Bitcoins simply by running a program on your computer.

This is one of the key reasons why this system has become wildly successful. As a miner, for each new coin you discover as your computer trolls through the system, you will be reward-ed. It is a highly popular way to earn money and support the system at the same time. Also, miners collect transaction fees each time they add a block to the Blockchain.

However, to do this, you must have the right hardware on hand. If you hope to become a cryptocurrency miner, then you will have to have more than just a simple computer to get the job done. Here is what you'll need:

- CPU

The CPU or the Central Processing Unit is the key component in your computer that handles the everyday processes that your system needs. Its primary purpose is to make the big deci-sions for your computer's functions. It is com-prised of the electronic circuitry and performs all the functions of a computer program.

While in the beginning, this was the only way to mine for currency, it was not the most effi-cient. While the CPU is no longer the primary way to mine cryptocurrency, it is still used to earn a little money on the network. Many miners will use their CPU to join a mining pool. By doing this, they can combine their computing power with others to earn money. The potential for earning will still be limited in this way, but if you're just interested in a few earnings, you can definitely garner a little cash this way.

- GPU

The GPU of a computer is responsible for the real heavy lifting a computer does. It manages the graphics processing and does all the complex mathematical computations involved in running videos. It is much faster than CPU mining and is considerably more powerful.

Many miners may have a system that maintains multiple GPU units to get the most power and speed possible.

- FPGA

The Field Programmable Gate Array is a piece of hardware that is solely dedicated to mining. It is considered to be the next level of mining as it has increased the speed and efficiency of mining many times over. An added bonus of setting up your mining platform using the FPGA is that it draws very little power and you can keep it running 24-hours a day earning your profit around the clock.

- ASIC

The last in a long line of mining technology is the ASIC (Application Specific Integrated Circuit chips. First introduced in 2013, they have been steadily improving with each passing year. Like the FPGA, they have only one job, and that is to mine 24/7.

When it comes to mining, speed is extremely important, and with new hardware like the FPGA and the ASIC, older and slower systems will never be able to compete. While you can still mine with CPUs and GPUs, your potential for profit in the world of mining will depend largely on how fast your computer can troll the network for those transactions.

Getting set up to mine for cryptocurrency doesn't have to be hard. Before you can do that, however, you need to decide if you're going to be a lone miner or join a pool. Depending on which avenue you choose to take you'll have to set up your mining business differently.

Let's start with the individual miner and how to get set up.

1. Set up your own virtual private server (VPS) to perform the mining. This should be set aside to only use for your mining operations

2. Access your VPS

3. Follow the commands to set up the system to start mining.

4. Start mining

It is important to know that the energy required to mine can be quite extensive, so many choose to join mining pools. While you won't make as much money as you would individually, you'll save on energy in the process.

You also have the option of installing specialized mining software that can run on your local machine and it can be run on as many servers as you want to speed up the process.

Once you're registered on your server, all you need is your email address you used to sign up and follow the commands. When all of that is in place, you're ready to start mining and make money.

One of the challenges for individual miners is the difficulty in finding those blocks. For some, it has taken years before they were able to generate a block and earn a piece of the pie so joining a pool is much more practical for those who don't mind sharing the reward. It will require a smaller investment but increase the rewards exponentially. You will earn an income on a more regular basis.

Getting paid for mining can also be a little confusing to work out. You have several options to choose from.

PPS (Pay per Share): This option gives you instant payouts for every share of the block that your system solves. The money is taken out of pool's balance and can be withdrawn immediately.

PROP (Proportional pay): This payment method divides up the rewards based on the number of shares each miner has found for the pool and pays it out proportionately.

BPM or the Slush Pool: This type of pool divides the reward based on who participated towards the end of a block rather than those who participated throughout.

There are several other methods of divvying up and paying out when you are a part of a pool. To get a better understanding of it and to help you find out which one works best for you, it is strongly suggested that you get the details from each pool before you join.

How Does Cryptocurrency Mining Work?

To understand mining, one must begin with understanding the Blockchain and how it works.

When you think of a Blockchain, it is best to try to visualize it as a public ledger that is constantly being updated every second. It is not under any central control, but as each transaction is completed, it is added to the ledger keeping a running total of everything that is happening with that particular cryptocurrency.

The miner's job is to find those Bitcoins, validate each transaction and record every completed transaction as a new block on the Blockchain.

To accomplish this, miners need to have the power to search these out.

How to Mine Your Cryptocurrency

Okay, now let's look at exactly how to find those blocks to add to the chain. There are several steps involved in the mining process.

1. *Spending*: When a user decides he wants to buy goods from another user he will use his wallet to send 1 Bitcoin to the seller.

2. *Announcement*: An announcement that 1 Bitcoin payment needs to go to the seller's wallet is broadcast to all the nodes or computers connected to the buyer's wallet.

3. *Propagation*: The nodes then look at the buyer's spend amount and com-

pares it to any other transactions that may still be pending. If they find no conflicts, the nodes broadcast the transaction to the entire network.

4. Miners will take their copy of the Blockchain and monitor for any new transactions that may be coming. He then works to fit all new and verified transactions into the block.

The miner who completes the work faster and provides his work test (the hash) actually receives the reward.

Every solved block receives a substantial reward.

5. *Confirmation*: The miner solves the block and he announces it to the network. If the other nodes are in agreement, the new block is added to the Blockchain, and the miner starts again looking for a new problem to solve.

6. *Notification*: The seller is notified and can now send his product to the buyer secure in knowing that the funds have been transferred successfully.

This process is pretty straightforward, but in some cases, it can become quite complicated. Especially in situations where large sums of money are being transferred where more than one confirmation may be necessary to ensure the validity of the transaction.

Chapter 7

CRYPTOCURRENCY EXCHANGES

As we have come to understand, cryptocurrencies are all digital in form so they all must be exchanged on a digital platform. A cryptocurrency exchange house works pretty much in the same manner as the stock market or the Forex market does. You can find professional brokers available, or you can opt to do your own trading online.

Since all transactions, therefore, must be completed online, these exchanges have several roles to play. First, they need to verify the identities of all participants relating to each transaction. This can be done through their social media accounts, their email accounts, or through a user account, they may hold on their exchange.

While most exchanges insist that users have verified accounts, others you will find are not very restrictive. It is up to you to decide which of these types of exchanges you will be most comfortable with. Keep in mind that those that do not require as much verification can conduct transactions faster but may not be as secure.

Let's talk a little bit about the different types of exchanges you have to choose from.

1.   Brokers

These are websites that are set up only for selling cryptocurrency. These sites set their own prices; so make sure you shop around to find the best deal.

2.   Trading Platforms

These solely work to bring buyers and sellers together. They usually earn their money by charging a service fee for every transaction they can help to make happen.

3.   Direct Trading Systems

These exchange houses can affect more complicated trades than the straight buy and sell transaction. For the more advanced investor that wishes to do more exchanges within the system (one currency for another, etc.) this is the place you want to go.

These traders do not have set prices for their currencies and are free to set their own prices as they wish.

It is clear that choosing the type of currency exchange can be very important for the investor.

While you may be excited and ready to jump right into the fray, it can help to slow down a bit and make sure you've done your research well before you make any final decision.

So how do you choose the right exchange house? Just like with any other investment tool you use, it pays to make sure of everything before you proceed. Do not just choose the one with the biggest name or the smaller fees but take the time to get all of your questions answered. Something you need to know:

1. Do they have a reputation of credibility?

2. How complicated is it to open an account?

3. Are they easily accessible from your geographic location?

4. What are their exchange rates?

5. What are their service fees?

6. How can you pay for their services?

Once you've started your research, it's a good bet that you'll have even more questions that need to be answered before you come to a final decision about which exchange house you want to work with.

Top 3 Cryptocurrency Exchanges and Platforms

Coinbase

Coinbase has the backing of millions of global customers and is one of the most well-known trading platforms in the world. It is pretty easy to use, investors can buy, store, and trade in Bitcoin, Ethereum, and Litecoin via a mobile wallet that can be downloaded to Android Smartphones or iPhones. You can also do peer-to-peer trades with other users with their Global Digital Asset Exchange subsidiary. Users in the US, UK, Canada, Europe, Australia, and Singapore can all have easy access to GDAX. As of now, there are no transfer fees for moving your currency from Coinbase to GDAX however, you may find that in some areas some currencies are not available.

It has a good reputation, excellent security, and the fees are reasonable. Coinbase transactions are also covered by their own insurance plan. Users may find that they lack customer support, their payment methods are few, and there are many countries where digital trade is not accepted with their currency.

Poloniex

Poloniex is a relatively new trading platform founded in 2014. However, it has already become one of the leading cryptocurrency exchange houses in the world. It offers a secure environment for trading over 100 different cryptocurrencies pairs and offers specialized tools and data analysis for the more experienced investor. Users will find a volume-tiered, maker-taker fee schedule for all trades. Fees can change depending on a number of different factors. Fees for makers can range of 0 to 0.15% and fees for takers can range for 0.10 to 0.25%. They do not charge extra for withdrawals.

Creating an account is fast and easy, the system is very user-friendly and with the low trading fees Poloniex does a high-volume of the trade so that users will find that they are always able to close a trade.

One caveat is that they do not have the fastest customer service position and there is no fiat support.

Kraken

When it comes to trade volume in Europe Kraken is the largest platform. It is a partner to the first cryptocurrency bank and allows you to buy, sell, and trade easily between Bitcoins, Euros, US Dollars, British Pounds, and Japanese Yen. Investors can also trade between other digital currencies besides the most common Bitcoin, Ethereum, Monero, Augur, Litecoin, Dogecoin, and Ripple.

They have a pretty solid reputation, have decent rates, and low transaction fees. You will also find great customer support and a secure and well-supported platform.

There may be limited options for payment methods, and if you are new to trading, it may not be the easiest platform to navigate for beginners.

Chapter 8

HOW TO STORE AND SECURE CRYPTO-CURRENCY

Even though cryptocurrency is digital in the format, it still needs to be stored in a safe place. When you have physical money, you usually can keep it in your wallet or open an account at the bank. For those with a lot of money on hand, a safe or another form of storage may be necessary.

When it comes to cryptocurrency, storage decisions may not be so simple. Every transaction made with cryptocurrency is kept on a Blockchain, which holds a number of wallets that are provided for account holders. But it is best to avoid thinking of these wallets in the same way you might think of a safe deposit box or a safe in a bank.

The wallet you have access to will have two addresses. The first address is a public one. This address or key is needed so that others can send you money when you sell. The private address is password protected and will give you access to your funds when you want to make a withdrawal or a deposit. The private key is also used to transfer funds to other account holders.

It is important to protect your private key above all else. View it like you would view any other important documents (social security number, passport number, etc.) It should never be revealed to anyone unless you want to give them access to your money.

Online wallet: The standard wallet for digital currency is the online wallet that you can easily access through your browser. It is strongly recommended that you do not put all your currency into your online wallet.

One of the reasons for this is because they become very tempting targets for hackers who will spend a lot of energy trying to break their codes and get into them.

Online wallets are usually the fastest way to complete any transaction, they are perfect for holding small sums of currency, and some can hold more than one currency at a time allowing you to transfer your money from one to the next.

However, they are often the target of phishing scams, malware, hacking, and other means of criminals might use to get around your security measures.

They often defeat the purpose of investing in cryptocurrency (to cut out the middleman) as they store information with a third-party.

Mobile Wallet: Mobile wallets are great for people who are constantly on the move. These work well from mobile devices so wherever you can get access to the Internet, you can make your transactions.

They tend to be more practical and convenient to use, and most can accept or send payments quickly. Some even have the ability to produce a QR code that can be scanned to complete a transaction.

Caution, however, is warranted because your smartphone is likely the least secure device in your arsenal. Phones can be compromised very easily, and even encryption software is not safe if your phone has been exposed to malware, keyloggers, or web viruses.

Desktop Wallet: Considered to be the safest of all wallets, desktop wallets have several advantages. They are probably the easiest to use and work as the ideal "cold storage" solution to housing your cryptocurrency. Cold storage simply means housing your keys offline where Internet hackers cannot get to it.

While it is considered to be the safest, desktop wallets are only as safe as the computer and Internet service you use. Without the proper security measures in place, your computer can be just as exposed as with any other type of wallet. Also, you must always remember to back up your computer because if for some reason it fails, your access to your currency dies with it.

Hardware Wallet: These are not as user-friendly as other wallets, but they are easy to use and more secure than a hot wallet (a wallet kept online). It works in the same way as a paper wallet (listed below) where your currency is stored offline. They have the same security as other wallets but are only vulnerable to criminal activity when connected online.

Hardware wallets have two parts; on that is connected to the Internet and the other that is not. The part that is connected to the Internet houses the public keys and performs all of the same functions of other wallets however it does not have access to the private key, so it cannot sign off on any transactions.

When you are ready to begin a transaction, you connect the offline device via a USB port or scan it in with a QR code to authorize and complete the transaction.

While it does have some vulnerabilities, it is considered to be the most secure way to store your cryptocurrency on a long-term basis. Still, it can be very tedious to use but is one of the most important tools to have when transferring large quantities of cryptocurrencies.

Paper Wallet: A great way to safely manage your cryptocurrency. It is an offline tool for storing your digital currency. A paper wallet allows you to print out your private keys and address onto physical paper. Depending on what security measures you have in place it can be one of the safest ways to avoid your currency being stolen by an outside hacker.

None of your keys are entered into the computer until you are ready to use them, and nothing is stored on a third-party server making it one of the safest ways to store your currency. It does, however, require much more work to trade currencies or move them around and it is more technical to fully grasp how to use it.

When choosing the right wallet, there are several things you need to keep in mind. Each wallet has its own pros and cons, so it is important to consider your personal needs when you choose. Here are just a few factors you might want to consider:

1. *Convenience*: Make sure that the wallet will be convenient for you to use when you need it. Choose something that will work with several different types of cryptocurrencies but also is compatible with a number of different software programs and exchange platforms.

2. *Accessibility*: You need to able to get to your coins when you need them. Make sure access is 24/7.

3. *Security*: Know the security protocols for your wallet. Check its history and look for any instances of hacking and what was done about it.

4. *Utility:* Your wallet should be user-friendly. Mistakes can be extremely costly when dealing with cryptocurrencies, and once transactions have been validated, there is no turning back.

5. *Cost:* Investors always look for transaction fees when they are thinking about crypto-currency, but you must also factor in the cost of storing your currency. There are many free wallets available with no costs but those wallets generally give you limited functions, but if you want to do more complex forms of trade, it is a good idea to find one with a monthly fee.

Since there is a variety of wallet options to choose from, it should not be difficult to find the one that will work best for your circumstances. Just keep in mind that every wallet has its own pros and cons, so make sure you factor all of that in before making a decision.

Chapter 9

6 MISTAKES TO AVOID WHILE TRADING CRYPTOCURRENCIES

There are many people now who are learning about cryptocurrencies and are ready to trade. However, as with all types of investments getting too emotionally involved, too excited about the venture can lead to trouble. You forget to take the necessary precautions, and you usually end up losing out in the end. Newcomers to the digital currency trade tend to make the same types of mistakes and end up in situations that they could have easily avoided if they had been forewarned. Here are the most common mistakes you should try to avoid when you start trading in the cryptocurrency market.

Weakly informed

No matter what your goals are or what you expect to get out of your investment strategy, knowledge can be your best friend, or it can be your worst enemy if you don't have it. It pays to do a lot of research before deciding to jump into the deep end. As you can see from what we've discussed already, it can be very easy to make money with cryptocurrency, but it can be very costly if you make a mistake.

Just the fact that once a block is set up on the Blockchain, it cannot be reversed or altered should be warning enough that mistakes can be extremely costly. People have lost thousands of dollars simply by inputting the wrong information, giving their code to the wrong people, or just not doing their homework and investing in the wrong type of currency.

Before you invest, always learn as much as you can about the currency, the protocols, the security in place, the fees, and anything else that may affect your return on investment. Learn the history of the currency, the exchange, the activity and always have a plan in place before you start.

Without regulatory conditions in place, you are solely responsible for what happens to your money. If you don't fully understand it or you're just making a decision based on what other people tell you, trouble is definitely waiting for you down the line.

Investing Without a Plan

This applies to any type of investment tool you plan to use, but it is even more important when dealing with cryptocurrency. Before you ever put a dollar into the market, you must have a strategy for how you're going to get it out.

Set rules for yourself that will help to remove the emotion from the trade. You should already have in mind under what conditions you plan to sell and the terms for when you need to get out of the market to cut your losses. Once you've started down that road to investing, decide what strategies you will take to improve your performance and your return on investment.

Use the history and data you found during your research to create a solid plan of action so that you're not caught later on having a knee-jerk reaction to a sudden change in the market.

Buying into Scams

There are many opportunities available when you're dealing with cryptocurrency, but there are also many opportunities to lose everything if you're not careful. New traders are often duped because they lack the experience or knowledge needed to distinguish between a legitimate trade and someone who is trying to pull the wool over their eyes.

In the beginning, try to avoid investing in new and unproven coins that have been "recently developed" and wait until they have established a solid reputation in the market.

Even when trading with well-known coins, look to purchase them at the lowest price possible from reputable exchange houses. It might even be better to wait until you are sure before you jump in. The wait may reduce your chances of a bigger profit, but it can also save you from buying a currency that has no profitability.

Leaving the Coins Unexchanged

Leaving your coins on the exchange is tantamount to expecting someone else to take care of your money. You might think that leaving your money in the exchange is the same as depositing it in the bank, but there is a huge difference.

When you deposit money in the bank, your account is FDIC insured, but with cryptocurrency, there is no such protection. Every day, hackers, scammers, and all sorts of people are trying to break the system.

Once you've made your investment and secured your profits, you should immediately transfer those funds to your private wallet (preferably maintained offline), which is protected by your private key. This way, only you and those you authorize have access to it.

Choosing the Wrong Exchange

All exchanges are not created equal, so it's important that you make your trades with an exchange designed to suit your purposes. This is also why it's good to conduct a thorough research and have a plan before you invest.

Some exchanges have a solid reputation and can be trusted while others may have a questionable history.

Choosing the wrong exchange can cause anything from problems getting your money out when you want it to not having access to it at all.

Having Your Finger in Too Many Pies

With so many currencies to choose from, it could be very tempting to dab a little here and try a little there hoping to hit the big time. But when you are trading too many altcoins at one time it can have a negative effect on your portfolio. For newcomers, it is best to start off with one or two currencies and then as you gain experience diversify more as you learn how to evaluate the risks.

These are not the only things you should be wary of when you invest in cryptocurrency. Consider this list just a start. There are many things you need to be watchful of, and as you learn the system, you'll soon learn how to identify various danger signs that could spell a trap where your money could fall through and end up out of your reach.

Even the most experienced of traders make mistakes from time to time, but the newcomer is especially vulnerable. Do your research and ask a lot of questions and you'll not only find the most profitable trades, but you'll also find you are more confident in your decisions, which could reduce the risk of impulsive and emotional trading that can be the cause of the trouble.

Chapter 10

THE PROS AND CONS OF CRYPTOCURRENCY

A cryptocurrency is a unique form of currency. It's ability to use encryption techniques to encode transactions sets it apart from any other currency we have ever used in the past. As it grows in popularity more and more people are becoming fascinated by this new innovation, and it is enticing people from all over the globe to get in on its high potential for profit.

When you speak with those who trade in this currency, it is likely that you hear many positive things about it. At the same time, you might hear many raise questions and doubts about its legitimacy. Like all other currencies, many good things can be said about it, but it is not all that glitter are gold either. There are many valid and legitimate claims that present genuine risks as well.

The Pros

There are many good things that we can list here, but we'll try to keep the list down to a reasonable size.

Transparency: When trading in digital currency all transactions are recorded and monitored. When a transaction has been completed, it is added to the ledger, and it becomes a permanent part of the record. This information cannot be manipulated or altered in any way. No individual or organization can change it making it one of the most secure of all transactions.

Since assets can be moved securely from one user to another, it significantly reduces the risk of fraud or tampering by outside parties.

Global Reach: No matter where you are in the world, if you have access to the Internet you can trade in cryptocurrency, but because it is not backed by any geographical boundaries or governmental institutions, it is accepted and used in most countries of the world. That cannot be said about any other traditional currency in the world.

Low Transaction Fees: The fact that the transaction fees for trading in cryptocurrency are a mere fraction of the fees that most financial institutions charge which makes it extremely appealing. The larger the transaction, the more you'll benefit from this as it can save you hundreds upon thousands of dollars.

Better Security: Unlike traditional payments, like cash and credit cards, cryptocurrencies are digital and encrypted; you cannot be ripped off in a transaction as you can be with legacy payment systems, and it is much harder to steal cryptocurrency compared to a full wallet cash. In a world where so many of our transactions are online, and our savings and credit rating are at stake at all times, anything that provides increased transactional security is a plus. And there is currently no transaction mechanism that is more safe and secure than those that use cryptocurrency.

You Control Your Money: Void of any middleman or third-party interests, no one is in charge of your money. There is no other electronic cash system in which your account isn't owned by someone else. Take PayPal, for example: if the company decides for some reason that your account has been misused, it has the power to freeze all of the assets held in the account, without consulting you. It is then up to you to jump through whatever hoops are necessary to get it cleared so that you can access your funds.

With cryptocurrency, you own the private key and the corresponding public key that makes up your cryptocurrency address. No one can take that away from you (unless you lose it yourself, or host it with a web-based wallet service that loses it for you).

Cons

Lack of Acceptance: One of the biggest negatives with cryptocurrencies is their newness. While users can do a lot of things with them; buy, sell, trade, or purchase but it is not like the whole world would accepts them like they do VISA or American Express. Finding vendors that are willing to accept crypto for the payment of goods and services is not always easy. Until it is, users will have to exchange their currency for local currency to make most purchases.

Volatile: While Bitcoin is a pretty stable currency, most other cryptocurrencies are not. When you are ready to invest, it is important to remember that it should be treated more like a commodity. Prices can fluctuate wildly depending on the flow of the market. If you view it more as a long-term investment, then you won't be sidetracked by the constant price fluctuations.

Cannot be Recovered if Lost: We've said it several times throughout the pages of this book. Cryptocurrencies cannot be recovered if they are lost. Unlike financial institutions that have regulations to protect your investment, a single incident of hacking could literally wipe you out.

For that reason, keeping your currency off the Internet when not in an active trade is the best way to protect your investment.

Still in Development: Cryptocurrency is a baby on the world's economic scene, and while it has a very promising future, it is very important that you keep it in perspective. It is still in development, and there will likely be many changes coming in the future. Investors must be prepared to accept and adapt to these changes before the system is fully perfected.

Chapter 11

SMART CONTRACTS

From the first introduction of Bitcoin, crypto-currency has been going through a major evolution with an endless stream of improvements with each new emerging currency. Smart contracts are just one of those evolutionary changes in a digital currency that has lots of advantages.

What Is a Smart Contract?

The term "smart contract" has no clear and settled definition.

The idea has long been hyped to the public as a central component of next-generation blockchain platforms, and as a key capability for any practical enterprise application.

They are defined variously as "autonomous machines," "contracts between parties stored on a blockchain" or "any computation that takes place on a blockchain." Many debates about the nature of smart contracts are really just contests between competing terminologies. The best way to describe smart contracts is to compare the technology to a vending machine. Ordinarily, you would go to a lawyer or a notary, pay them, and wait while you get the document. With smart contracts, you simply drop a bitcoin into the vending machine (i.e., ledger), and your escrow, driver's license, or whatever drops into your account. More so, smart contracts not only define the rules and penalties around an agreement in the same way that a traditional contract does, but also automatically enforce those obligations.

Another way to understanding smart contracts is to realize that these are digital versions of real contracts. With a standard contract between two parties, you have an agreement that stipulates what each party must do for the transaction to be completed. The contract actually sets the parameters of who does what, when to do it, how to do it, and what happens once it's been done.

Up until Smart Contracts, these agreements have only been in verbal or written form subjected to territorial laws and regulations of the land where they were drawn up. Also, with these contracts, the terms of the contract could always subject to interpretation.

Today's Smart Contracts improve on all of that. Firstly, these digital agreements are designed to be self-executing and enforced without any additional party to weigh in on the matter. There is no need to have the language of the agreement interpreted in any way.

Rather than writing them in spoken language, Smart Contracts are written in computer code and programming languages that stipulate the terms and expectations of the agreement.

There are many advantages to this form of coded contracts that you may not readily recognize. These contracts do not need a company or regulations to enforce them. This means that there is no longer a bureaucracy or any associated costs for such services. They can actually be something like a do-it-yourself contract allowing them to self-manage based on the terms agreed upon by only the parties involved. Basically, you could look at them as programmable money, allowing users to solve common problems themselves.

Several cryptocurrencies are already using smart contracts including Bitcoin, Ethereum, and Lisk. However, this is only the beginning. Smart contracts are so efficient and practical that more currencies will be adopting them as the world of cryptocurrency continues to grow and expand.

How You Can Use Smart Contracts

Jerry Cuomo, vice president for blockchain technologies at IBM, believes smart contracts can be used all across the chain from financial services to healthcare to insurance.

Here are some examples:

Government

Insiders vouch that it is extremely hard for our voting system to be rigged, but nonetheless, smart contracts would allay all concerns by providing an infinitely more secure system. Ledger-protected votes would need to be decoded and require excessive computing power to access. No one has that much computing power, so it would need God to hack the system! Secondly, smart contracts could hike low voter turnout. Much of the inertia comes from a fumbling system that includes lining up, showing your identity, and completing forms. With smart contracts, volunteers can transfer voting online, and millennials will turn out en masse to vote for their Potus.

Management

The blockchain not only provides a single ledger as a source of trust, but also shaves possible snarls in communication and workflow because of its accuracy, transparency, and automated system. Ordinarily, business operations have to endure a back-and-forth, while waiting for approvals and for internal or external issues to sort themselves out. A blockchain ledger streamlines this.

It also cuts out discrepancies that typically occur with independent processing, and that may lead to costly lawsuits and settlement delays.

Automobile

There's no doubt that we're progressing from slothful pre-human vertebrates to super-smart robots. Think of a future where everything is automated. Google's getting there with smartphones, smart glasses, and even smart cars. That's where smart contracts help. One example is the self-autonomous or self-parking vehicles, where smart contracts could put into play a sort of 'oracle' that could detect who was at fault in a crash; the sensor or the driver, as well as countless other variables. Using smart contracts, an automobile insurance company could charge rates differently based on where, and under which, conditions customers are operating their vehicles.

Chapter 12

HOW CRYPTOCURRENCY CAN AND WILL DISRUPT THE FINANCIAL SYSTEM

Over the years, we have seen the global economy spiral downward in almost every country in the world. With all money being tightly regulated by the government and controlled by massive financial institutions, its negative effects have been felt in almost every sector.

Just the simple fact that these large conglomerates will not have any influence on the use of these currencies. They can and will take a huge burden off of many people. Aside from the obvious, the elimination of huge fees will make a tremendous difference in what happens to our economy in the future. But there are other advantages to cryptocurrencies that you may not even realize.

1. *Financial Integration*: One of the biggest changes to the global economy will be an equalizing of funds across the world. Without these institutions managing and monitoring everything, more people will have a say in how their money is earned or spent. This can spread to numerous underprivileged countries where corporations dictate to less advantaged people what they can buy and how they can use it. Now, with

peer-to-peer transactions made between only the parties involved, even the smallest user will have more say on how to spend or make their money.

2. *The Elimination of a Hierarchical System*: People will have more freedom of choice. Many people will be able to work online and no longer have to be forced to work for minuscule wages offered only in their immediate community. With Smart Contracts, they can dictate the terms of their own income and live in areas where they can avoid a life of poverty.

3. *Remittances*: When you think of the millions of people who are refugees, or disadvantaged persons who have been forced to immigrate to other countries to make enough money to get by, you must also think of the billions of dollars they send from one country to the next (estimated to be more than $550 billion). Then you think of the enormous fees that they must pay to send the money to their home. With cryptocurrencies, they can now make those transactions themselves and avoid many of those fees in the process. The amount of money saved will be astronomical. Imagine what good could come of that money when it is put back into the economy rather than in the pockets of corporations.

4. *Disruption of Infrastructure*: As crypto-currency is so adaptable in time, it will change the way we exchange value in many ways. While many people are still attached to the old system, as more people learn the benefits of cryptocurrency, they will defi-nitely want to switch. With its promise of more security, more privacy, and more freedom of choice, it will eventually change the way we buy, sell, and do all sorts of transactions in the future.

While the idea of switching to cryptocurrency is still pretty scary to many people, the more you learn about it, the more you'll see its po-tential. It is a powerful currency that is not going to go away and eventually it will erode this current economic system in a way that will change the very core of how we do business in every corner of this planet.

Chapter 13

WAYS TO MAKE MONEY WITH CRYPTOCURRENCY

For years, many people have been interested in investing in the stock market, mutual funds, Federal Bonds, IRAs, and all sorts of investment tools. In many cases, they have been prevented because the capital to get into these instruments is often out of reach for the average person. This keeps the profit potential squarely in the hands of the wealthy with only a few others getting in the privilege.

All of that changes when you're looking at making money with cryptocurrency. One would be very surprised at what they can do with just a small investment of a few dollars. Without expensive broker fees, commission paid to middlemen, and no minimum investment requirement even the average Joe will be able to turn a few dollars in short order.

Here are just a few ways you can make money using cryptocurrency.

1. Bitcoin Trading

Probably the easiest way to make money is by trading Bitcoin. With Bitcoin, you can trade with every other cryptocurrency on the market. All you need to do is buy the Bitcoin, scour the market for a better price and then sell it again. When trading with other currencies, always make sure you're trading for a currency you can sell later. When the price reaches a point where you can turn a profit, simply sell it and reap the rewards

2. Lending- Loan some bitcoins, earn some interest

Lending is perhaps the oldest way to use the money to make money. Basically, you loan out money to a relevant party, and they pay you back, with interest. Interest rates will vary with the risk involved. If you get collateral in exchange for your loan, interest rates will be low. No collateral means higher risks, but it also means higher interest rates.

3. Peer to peer lending

You can also do peer-to-peer lending online. You can literally become your own bank and choose who you'd like to invest your money in. With Smart Contracts, you can even set your own terms and conditions for the loans and then receive regular payments from your benefactor with interest.

4. Selling products and services

If you already have a business, you can sell your products or services online and accept Bitcoin or another cryptocurrency as payment.

5. Investing

Many people new to the market choose to buy Bitcoin and hold onto it for the long term. While the price fluctuates greatly from day to day, the overall trend has been consistently on the rise. The longer you hold onto it, the better your chances of a larger return on your investment.

6. Cloud Mining

Cloud Mining is the process of bitcoin mining utilizing a remote datacenter with shared processing power. Mining Bitcoin is a very active way to make money with cryptocurrency. With the right hardware and the time, you can generate a steady stream of income over an extended period of time.

Chapter 14

THE FUTURE OF CRYPTOCURRENCY

When Bitcoin was first introduced, many people could not see a future for it. This is understandable as it is often hard to envision something that has never been dreamed up before.

Davide Menegaldo, COO at Helperbit, said:

"I would imagine this scenario: in the future financial instruments linked to bitcoin will be finally approved. High finance will invest into the cryptocurrency (more than the 300M expected for the bitcoin ETF approval). I'm thinking about 5-10 times the current price. Bitcoin will not necessarily be used as a method of payment (it also depends on how the size block / Segregated witness / LN matter will proceed or will not), but primarily it will be used as a store of value. However, there will be much more competition as a payment method because some banks could issue their own cryptocurrency, while the current ones will remain a handful. Ethereum will consolidate as the second most important infrastructure, and 99% of ICO tokens will have any value."

Today, however, the dream is now beginning to take hold and it is growing at an exponential rate. It is hard to ignore the profit potential, the amount of freedom, and the financial independence that these digital currencies can bring. But many are wondering if this pipe dream is going to last and what does the extended future really hold for all of us.

It stands to reason that there will always be some who will hold out and try to maintain the status quo but for the most part, the future of these currencies are very promising. While governments have done little more than tolerate these innovative assets that news is spreading. In the midst of ridicule, naysayers, and disbelievers, cryptocurrency has become a relatively stable investment instrument that has provided an equalizing to its users.

One only needs to look at its history to be able to see what is in the store for the future. From its all-time low of $2 in the fall of 2011 to today's high of more than $3,800 in 2017, it is easy to see that in spite of all the complainers, whiners, naysayers, and such, Bitcoin is still climbing.

In its beginning years, it was very unstable, but there have always been supporters who have stuck with it and will continue to ride the wave for the foreseeable future.

Conclusion

Thank you so much for reading through the book that ought to help you understand the world of cryptocurrency, and the steps you can take to make money trading cryptocurrencies.

I hope it was useful to you and you got to understand the way cryptocurrency is changing the financial system and its impact on everyday life.

Just because you have finished reading this book doesn't mean that it stops here. You are required to expand your horizons if you want to learn more about cryptocurrency. When done, stop reading and think of how you can implement the things you have learnt in real life and improve your living standard.

Finally, before you go, I'd like to say "thank you" for purchasing my book.

I know you could have picked from dozens of books on this topic, but you took a chance with my guide. So, big thanks for downloading this book and reading all the way to the end.

Additional Resources

www.deepdotweb.com/2017/04/30/tutorial-altcoin-flipping-cryptocurrency-trading-strategies-always-win/

www.bitcoinmagazine.com/articles/digital-vs-virtual-currencies-1408735507/

www.forbes.com/sites/kashmirhill/2014/01/31/bitcoins-legality-around-the-world/#680882a03ccd

www.theweek.com/articles/465541/want-make-money-bitcoin-mining-hint-dont-mine

www.cryptocoinsnews.com/altcoin/

www.cryptocurrencyfacts.com/how-does-cryptocurrency-work-2/

www.cryptocurrencyfacts.com/understanding-hard-forks-cryptocurrency/

www.cryptocurrencyfacts.com/how-to-send-and-receive-cryptocurrency/

www.cryptocurrencyfacts.com/how-to-trade-cryptocurrency-for-beginners/

www.cryptocurrencyfacts.com/maker-vs-taker-cryptocurrency/

BLOCKCHAIN

Everything You Need to Know
About Blockchain Technology
and How It Works

Introduction

Congratulations on downloading *Blockchain: Everything You Need to Know About Blockchain Technology and How It Works* and thank you for doing so. Blockchain technology is already being called the most important new technology since the creation of the internet, despite the fact that only a small fraction of the population uses it on a regular basis. As such, you are now in a unique position to be at the forefront of the biggest technological expansion of the decade.

Some of the specifics can be a bit opaque, however, which is why the following chapters will take it slow and start out by discussing the basics of blockchain and describing how it works in simple terms so that everything is on the same page when it comes to the details. This information will then be built upon with a discussion of how blockchain technology can be used successfully along with its pros and cons. Next, you will learn all about how blockchain technology is on track to reshape financial services and why cryptocurrency is so important to a wide swath of the globe.

From there you will learn about several different apps that are well on their way to shaping the future before taking a more in-depth look at the specifics behind blockchain. Then you will learn about how business is likely to change in the blockchain era, and how to successfully implement the blockchain technology in your business. Finally, you will learn about the industries that blockchain is most likely to disrupt in the next decade and what the future is likely to hold for this versatile technology.

There are plenty of books on this subject on the market, thanks again for choosing this one! Every effort was made to ensure it is full of as much useful information as possible. Please enjoy!

Chapter 1

Introducing Blockchain

If you have heard the phrase blockchain, but you cannot say much on the subject other than it is connected to bitcoin in one way or another then do not worry, you are not alone. In fact, a vast majority of Americans cannot define a blockchain and less than 2 percent use one on a regular basis. While the adoption rate might be low at the moment, there is a reason those who are familiar with this technology are already calling it the most important new technology since the creation of the internet. So the sooner you learn about it, the sooner you can start using it to your advantage.

At its most basic, a blockchain is a type of decentralized database that works as a type of ledger for financial transactions. Due to the way it is secured, it is both easy for authorized users to access and very difficult for unauthorized users to access, for reasons that will be explained in detail in the later chapters. As the name implies, a blockchain is made up of individual blocks that each contains unique transaction information as well as information relating to his or her unique place in the chain. Every time a new block is added to a blockchain from an authorized node, that information is then shared with all the other nodes that make up the network after it has been verified. No centralized authority needs to tell the nodes to seek new information.

When it comes to security, the blockchain does not take any offensive measures against threats and instead relies on extreme defense to win the day. As transactions need to be verified before they are added to the primary blockchain, any malicious blocks that may be sent will be automatically picked up and discarded before they can infect the whole blockchain. Only when all of its data lines up with at least 51 percent of all other nodes, a new block will be added to the blockchain. While, technically, it is possible to generate enough fabricated cloud to add a fake block to a chain, the resources required to do so are beyond the means of modern hackers and the costs for doing so would outstrip the gains.

In addition to storing information, the blockchain automatically timestamps the data which means it is extremely easy to determine when a given transaction took place after the fact. When all of its facets are taken together, it becomes easy to see why blockchains can essentially act autonomously with new blocks being created and assigned, and the whole being policed for errors, without anyone actively stepping in and taking control over any of it.

Humble Beginnings

The earliest versions of what would go on to be

blockchain technology was created in the 1980s by a programmer who was looking for a wait to stop spam email from clogging up his inbox. The impetus for what would eventually become blockchain technology is a proof of work model which is essentially a math problem that gets harder and harder, the more times it is called upon to verify details at once. As such, solving the equation to send a single email was something that 1980s computers could handle, solving it 10,000 times to send out a spam email was not. This same proof of work model is used in modern blockchain technology and explains why individual transactions need to be verified.

After its creation, the proof of work model only saw limited use until 2008 where it started gaining traction as a hypothetical means of facilitating a digital type of currency that wouldn't be bound by the traditional financial framework in an online peer-to-peer forum. While it was just a talk at this point, one of the members of the discussion, someone or a group of people using the alias Satoshi Nakamoto, took the conversation more serious than the rest and went to work creating the original design document for blockchain technology, and bitcoin as well, called *bitcoin: A P2P Electronic Cash System,* along with the code that would become the basis of the modern bitcoin blockchain. With proof of their ideas in hand, many new programmers jumped on the blockchain bandwagon, and soon the Nakamoto alias was never heard again.

To understand the ins and outs of how block-chain works, it is necessary to understand a bit more about how bitcoin works as well. Broadly speaking, it can be thought of as similar to other online payment systems such as PayPal. The biggest difference here is the fact that the currency does not have a real-world analog that the digital version is standing in for. The value of the currency is based purely on what the marketplace has decided, and what investors are willing to pay for it.

Each of the transactions made through the system then forms the blocks of the blockchain that keeps bitcoin on its feet. Transactions are then verified by individuals who are paid for their time in portions of a single bitcoin. The number of transactions that can be verified on the bitcoin blockchain is already being pushed up against which leaves many analysts wondering if another cryptocurrency is going to come along and take its crown. These individuals use very specialized computers, known as bitcoin mining machines, to complete proof of work problems that are infinitely more advanced than what would have passed for security in the 1980s. In fact, the proof of work that is required for the average block these days is so complicated that one specialized machine is not enough, so miners have to group together to complete them in a reasonable period of time. When this occurs, the group of miners then split the reward. While this might not seem like much, a single bitcoin was worth more than $4,000 in September 2017.

In 2014, when bitcoin was first making a big splash amongst mainstream investors, programmers learned how to add a unique type of code to individual blocks to allow them to carry out specific tasks.

This type of code is known as smart contracts, and they are discussed in detail in a later chapter.

Smart contracts are useful in a wide variety of scenarios, from facilitating contract negotiation to tracking patients in a hospital and their inclusion in the blockchain bag of tricks has cemented it as a technology to watch moving forward.

Since 2014, the cryptocurrency market has exploded, and thus the blockchain market with it as one cannot exist without the other. As of September 2017, there are more than 1,000 different cryptocurrencies on the market, varying in price from thousands of dollars all the way down to 1 cent or less. Collectively, they have a market cap of an estimated 60 billion dollars which puts them in the company of major corporations such as Tesla, Boeing, and Microsoft.

Along with this boom has come an influx of new technologies to take advantage of the burgeoning marketplace, the best of which are discussed in later chapters.

Chapter 2

HOW DOES THE BLOCKCHAIN TECHNOLOGY WORK – IN PLAIN ENGLISH

So, now that we have spent some time discussing blockchain and some of the benefits that come with this technology, it is time to understand how this type of technology is going to work. It is pretty simple for users to use this kind of technology, it only takes a few minutes to do transactions and you are signed up automatically when you join in on a digital currency. However, the things that happen behind the scenes are a bit more complex, which helps to provide the trust and security that the system needs.

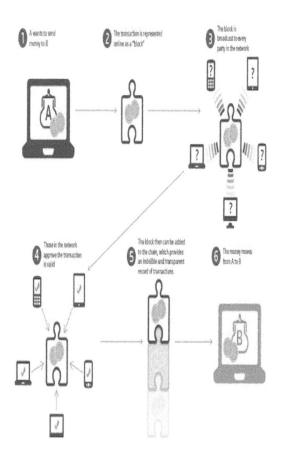

1. A wants to send money to B

2. The transaction is represented online as a "block"

3. The block is broadcast to every party in the network

4. Those in the network approve the transaction is valid

5. The block then can be added to the chain, which provides an indelible and transparent record of transactions

6. The money moves from A to B

Since we will mostly associate blockchain with Bitcoin and some of the other digital currencies that are out there, it is easiest to take a look at how blockchain will work on these networks. It will work similarly on other networks as well, but this will help to keep things in order. On the blockchain, when you complete a transaction, it will end up showing up, in order, on one of the blocks you are using. When the block is filled up, it will join in the permanent record and will link together with the other blocks that you have completed to form a chain. This all works together to help keep your information in order and keeps it secure from others who may want to take a look at the information.

Each block in the blockchain is going to be responsible for holding onto all the important information about the transactions that you've completed and each of the blocks will hold onto a lot of data. Depending on the network that you work with, these blocks could contain information about currencies, digital rights, identity, and property titles to name a few. Since these blocks can hold onto so much information and will keep that information safe, blockchain is one of the best ways to help people interact, send money, and even make their purchases.

When you decide to join the Bitcoin network, and you create your own Bitcoin address, you will join in on its blockchain. Each user will receive a block that they will be able to fill up each time they finish a new transaction. These blocks can hold onto quite a bit of information, and some people will fill them up quickly, and others may take a bit longer.

After the block has been filled up with the different transactions that you are working on, they are going to become a part of the permanent record on Bitcoin. They will join the Bitcoin network's blockchain, and you will start making your own personal blockchain which will just contain all of the blocks that contain your own transactions.

When one block is all filled up, it is time to receive another block, which the system will automatically send over to you. You can then start to fill up that block with transactions as well, and the process keeps going for as long as you keep using the network. Every user on the Bitcoin network, or whatever platform you are using at the time, will have their own blockchain that is full of personal transactions. But as the blocks fill up, those will be added to the permanent blockchain that the Bitcoin network relies on, so the information is kept safe. This process works together to make sure the Bitcoin network remains transparent to use.

This can all seem a little bit confusing right now, but one way to think about how blockchain works is to think of it as your own bank statement. Each block you receive will be like a monthly statement that you get from the bank. You can look over it to see what transactions you have completed in recent times and check to make sure it is all good. After you have finished a few of these statements, they will all become part of your bank history. They will be a part of your permanent record with the bank (or regarding the blockchain, with the Bitcoin network), and you can always look back to see what payments you have made, what funds you have received, and any other transaction. The main difference between them is that blockchain is going to be online and will only be in charge of things that happen on the Bitcoin network.

One nice thing that comes with the blockchain technology is that it works with Bitcoin to keep your transactions safe and secure. There are some special codes or some hashes that will be added in so that hackers and other people will not be able to steal your information. Anyone who is on the network can see these transactions, but they will have to look through these special hashes to see what is going on. It is the work of the miners on the Bitcoin network that will make sure the blockchain ledger is secure, and they will be rewarded with 25 Bitcoin each time that they are successful.

The job of the miner may sound easy, but some complications can come with it and they are in charge of maintaining most of the security of this system. They will need to come up with the unique hashes that will help to hide up all of your information so that it will be safe from others who want to look. But they cannot just go through and write out any random number that they would like, or anyone could do this, and all of the coins on Bitcoin would be mined.

Instead, there are a few rules to the hashes that are created. First, the beginning of each hash needs to have a certain number of zeroes, and since you do not know how a hash will look until you are done, you could create quite a few of these before getting the results. Also, the hashes have to be designed so that if any one character in the chain is changed, it is going to change up all of the characters that come after it as well. This makes it complicated to make a good hash, but it does make it easier to catch if someone has been messing around in the blockchain.

As you can guess, the process of creating one of these codes is not the easiest, but these rules ensure that your information is going to stay safe and not just anyone could add in a random code to the mix. If they could do that, then a code could do the work, and the security would be gone. Right now, the miners will be rewarded with 25 Bitcoin when they are done. Since Bitcoin is worth about $3200 right now, this can be a good reward for the work they are doing. This becomes a win-win situation for everyone who is involved. The miners will get paid well for the work that they are doing, and the users of the network can rest assured that their information will stay safe.

The blockchain is a really neat piece of technology that has so many potential applications for users to enjoy. Right now, it is the leading force that has helped Bitcoin become so popular, but it is sure to change many other aspects of our world in the future. It is such a simple idea, just a ledger to keep track of transactions, but it is so efficient and easy to use that many platforms for different applications are already in use.

Chapter 3

HOW CAN BLOCKCHAIN TECHNOLOGY BE USED?

In Business

Dealing with money: While blockchain and cryptocurrency already go hand in hand, there is still more to what can be done when it comes to blockchain meeting the needs of most businesses. The Ethereum Enterprise Alliance is an organization that is dedicated to ensuring that this changes as quickly as possible. It is comprised of over 100 member organizations including the likes of Samsung, Microsoft, and JP Morgan and is focused on the goal of adapting the technology behind the Ethereum platform to more appropriately suit the needs of major corporations.

Fraud prevention: Fraud regularly costs business owners as much as a third of their profits on a yearly basis. Blockchain technology can help decrease this rate due to the way it can track identities online that is both secure and efficient. Blockchain can easily cut down on false identification requests and the results it provides are always going to be immutable, authenticated, irrefutable and secure. This type of system could easily function with dual factor authentication or constantly changing passwords in favor of a system of cryptography and digital signatures to keep everyone in their place at all times.

With this type of system, transactions can normally be processed, and the only check against the blockchain that will be required is at the point where the funds are moved between accounts. A variant of the technology will also be used when it comes to providing passports, birth certificates, account details, residency forms and ID cards. There are already applications in circulation that can work successfully as an alternative to a traditional passport.

Improving supply chains: One area where many companies have traditionally stumbled is when it comes to the extreme level of detail management that is required to ensure their supply chain is running smoothly. Blockchain technology can make this entire process significantly more manageable by automating a vast majority of the steps that are required when transferring large amounts of goods between locations. Through the use of smart contracts, companies will be able to easily track their products door to door, thanks to shipping containers that are internet enabled with signatures being obtained digitally and payments being made in the same way.

Massive public ledger: The Ethereum Enterprise Alliance is currently working on a blockchain that will serve as a public ledger for the blockchains of a wide variety of products and items to interact with one another. This ledger would serve as a sort of bridge that would make all the various blockchains that are connected to it more effective without adding much regarding costs. Devices attached to this public ledger would then be able to communicate autonomously, saving energy, issuing updates and correcting errors in the process.

Funding: Thanks to blockchain, new companies are going to have even more ways to fund their startup dreams. 4G Capital is a company that is already using blockchain as a means of facilitating small business loans to business owners in Africa. Through the Ethereum blockchain, donors can connect to recipients directly and provide them with the funds they need via a proprietary transaction system. Furthermore, in addition to providing loans for 100 percent of the asking price, in an unsecured fashion, it gives those who would otherwise not be able to get loans access to funds that are literally life-changing.

While currently operating in a limited fashion, as this idea catches on, it has the potential to change a vast swath of the financial sector.

In Media and Marketing

Promotional cards: It does not matter if the card is for a free sandwich after five purchases or for ten percent off all future orders, these types of cards, along with gift cards, are a great way to get the name of a company in front of the customer whenever they open their wallet. Unfortunately, these cards are very easy to lose, negating the potential value gained from creating a habit amongst customers. Blockchain technology has the potential to revolutionize this space by connecting customers to various loyalty programs directly through a blockchain which can then update the customer's relevant details as needed.

Microblogging: When it comes to interacting with their target audience as quickly and effectively as possible, blockchain technology is offering businesses even more ways to stay in touch. Projects such as EthTweet show the potential for microblogging from a blockchain platform by providing microblogging options via the Ethereum blockchain. The service is much the same as Twitter, except because it is decentralized, it is impossible to pressure anyone to take down content or to take it down yourself once it is part of the blockchain, it is there for good.

Enhanced advertising: Comcast is already working on a new technology that is powered by blockchain that lets advertisers make ad buys via their own private blockchain. Furthermore, the company also allows programmers, publishers and marketers share the data with one another without having to actually pool it in a single location. For example, this service allows a marketer to be able to access data from a content producer to better understand how to target ad buys for that particular program or type of content.

Whitelisting: The company MetaX runs a blockchain registry in collaboration with ConsenSys and DMA that pays users in the cryptocurrency adToken to help them determine which content publishers can be considered reputable. Advertisers then have access to this data when it comes to making advertising buying decisions.

Ad buying: Nasdaq is partnering with a company called the New York Interactive Advertising Exchange to provide a place for agencies, publishers, and brands to sell or buy future ad inventory starting in late 2017. The idea here is for contract execution to be automated via a mixture of blockchain reliance and smart contracts.

In Property

Notary services: The way that a given blockchain verifies information, it could naturally serve as a stand-in for notary services. In fact, there are already numerous different apps on the market that provide notary services based on blockchain technology.

Enhanced property rights: All forms of intangible and tangible property will eventually be connected via blockchain and smart contract technology. Everything from houses and cars to patents and ownership shares will all be cataloged and tracked, making the concept of ownership rights much more concrete than it often is now. These sorts of details will all be stored in a decentralized ledger along with any relevant contractual details, and the blockchain and smart contracts in question will even be able to generate smart keys that allow access to a specific property at specific times.

The same thing goes for the way in which relevant documents are handled. This includes things like birth, death and marriage certificates and all the various privileges and rights they come with. This will be a dramatic improvement over the current system where these details are often not stored properly or treated with the respect they deserve. So much so that UNICEF estimates that 30 percent of children under the age of five do not have an accurate birth certificate. Creating a blockchain that can keep track of these details will not only make tracking these types of services much more manageable, but it will also make it easier for individuals to track down their personal documents as well.

Finally, with the right groundwork, your blockchain identification could even replace the several different forms of identification you currently have to carry around on a regular basis. The blockchain ID could replace your driver's license, your business ID card, your passport, your social security card and more. This ledger will be accessible from anywhere in the world, and it will contain all the details you would ever need to prove your identity beyond the shadow of a doubt.

This identification system wouldn't stop in the real world. However, it would also track your activities in digital space, for good or for ill. Currently, it can be difficult to know whom to trust online, but if everyone you met came with an aggregate score based on all their online interactions, you would likely find it much easier to know who you would be comfortable associating with. Unlike with current forms of social media, the blockchain version would make it impossible for those with negative scores to remove anything about themselves, ensuring that they have to live with the consequences of their online actions.

Take ownership of the power your home produces: Blockchain technology, combined with increasingly cost-effective solar power options, is working to decentralize the power grid. Rather than require a centralized provider, through this system individual power their homes with solar panels and high-capacity batteries and then sell off whatever they do not personally use. Those who are in need of power could draw it from those who have an excess, and the payment and authorization to do so would all be handled via blockchain technology and smart contracts.

To Secure Sensitive Data Storage

Online storage: When it comes to digital storage, blockchain is providing an interesting solution to an old problem that is already being used to connect users with other people's cloud storage space. In this case, the blockchain is an intermediary between users looking for storage space and those with storage space to spare, and the service works much the way Airbnb does. Estimates put the amount spent on cloud storage so far at more than 20 billion dollars, so this could be a profitable opportunity for lots of people if the idea catches on.

Revitalized internet: These days, the internet is a much more centralized place than it once was. One startup company by the name of Blockstack is looking to take it back to its decentralized roots. During the second half of 2017, it plans to release an internet browser that will allow those with access to blockchain technology to access a variation of the standard internet where users have almost complete control of all of their data.

This will work mostly the same as they do now, except that once users are finished interacting with a given site or service, they will have the option to remove their data from that site completely. Additionally, login details will be stored on the blockchain so one account name and password will be enough to access all of your personalized content. Microsoft is already working hard to add this technology to its own browser.

Increase the security of pertinent data: Blockchain technology is already being put to work securing the records of entire countries. Currently, the company Factom is working with the country of Honduras in updating their land registration practices and with the Chinese government to get its prototype smart cities up and running.

Blockchain will be an integral part of this system when it comes to getting all the various types of systems communicating with one another.

Part of this system is also a notarization service for data along with an information management paradigm far beyond what is available to the public. Factom has also already received funding from the US Department of Homeland Security, specifically the Technology and Science Directorate to work on the Blockchain Software to Prove Integrity of Captured Data project.

Chapter 4

THE PROS AND CONS OF BLOCKCHAIN TECHNOLOGY

Pros

There are so many different reasons why you would want to use blockchain for yourself. Some people like to go into it to invest their time and money and earn something in return. On the other hand, lots of people will choose to go into blockchain because it just makes trade easier to work with than the traditional system. Either way, there are quite a few benefits that both parties can work with whether they want to ensure that their information stays safe online, they want to make sure that the government cannot mess with the money, or they just want to get their transactions done quickly. Let's take a look at some of the best benefits that you will experience when it comes to using this blockchain technology.

Transparency: When a system is based on the blockchain technology, they already can offer improvements in transparency, especially when they are compared to some of the other record keeping methods. When changes are made on this ledger, it is possible for each person who is on the network to see these changes. And once someone adds information to the blockchain, the transactions will not be changed or altered at all.

Our current record keeping methods are just not able to keep up with this. It is easier for someone to get onto these ledgers and they can pretty much make any alterations that they would like to the database, often without any of the users having any idea. On some of the larger ledgers, it could take a long time to ever catch on to some of the alterations. This is why there are big examples of fraud in our current system, and it is really hard to catch the person who performed such act.

Anyone who goes onto a network that uses blockchain will be able to see how transparent this kind of technology can be. All the computers that connect to the blockchain, which will happen when you join the network, will need to be there to approve any changes that are proposed on the blockchain. This makes it really hard for any transaction to be hidden or manipulated at all on the network. All of these changes are going to be done in real time so that they can quickly be placed back on the blockchain. While it is still possible that fraud could happen, it is much less likely compared to other methods that we use because this system is transparent.

It is possible to use blockchain technology to move some of this transparency to other industries as well. For example, there are already several big businesses that realize how valuable the transparency of blockchain is and they are working on implementing it for themselves. No matter what kind of industry you are working with, blockchain could provide you with the results that you need.

Get rid of the intermediaries: In our traditional way of doing things, most transactions are going to involve two parties and then they would also have an intermediary that would work with them. These intermediaries are supposed to be there to add in some trust to all transactions, but they also add in some high fees for the work that they do. This is why one of the benefits of using blockchain is that you can get rid of these intermediaries, while still having the trust that is needed. This will save both parties a lot of money in the process.

As you can imagine, there can be some great benefits to kicking out your intermediary. You will have trust in the system, and you will not have to worry about the third-party learning about your information and leaking it to other people for their own gains. You can finish up your transactions quickly because only two parties need to deal with it rather than three. And then both parties will enjoy that they will have fewer fees to pay as they do not have to pay the intermediary in this process.

Decentralization: The blockchain platform is considered decentralized, which is one of the reasons that it is so successful at getting rid of the intermediaries and remaining trustworthy and transparent for its users. Unlike our traditional banking system where each bank or financial institution has its own ledger that they need to reconcile (which really slows down the process), blockchain is going to be all done on one shared ledger. The company will be able to use blockchain without having to give up all of their control to a single institution, but since it is all on one ledger, it is much easier to keep all of the transactions in line, and they can be completed faster.

However, there are a few things that need to happen before this is going to work. First, all of the financial institutions will need to learn how to work together rather than seeing each other as competitors. Right now, most banks are going to have their own system that they like to use, and this slows down the process since each company has to do the work in their books when the transaction finishes. On the other hand, when you use a blockchain ledger, this will not be an issue because it will include one ledger, rather than two or more, which speeds up the process.

Trust: We have mentioned this one a few times, but the idea that blockchain can build up trust is so important to why people will complete transactions on this technology. The reason why blockchain is so effective is that it has found a way to build up trust between all the parties that work on a transaction. However, this kind of trust is currently found on the network, without having to involve a third party into the mix at all.

One of the reasons that there is a lot of trust inside the blockchain network is that the whole system is transparent. When you join a network that uses blockchain, you will instantly be able to see each transaction that occurs on the network, whether it is your own transactions or all other transactions. And the security that is placed on this network is meant to help make sure that information cannot be changed or manipulated, which helps to build up the levels of trust that people have inside of the system.

Security: When someone chooses to place data on the record of the blockchain, whether he or she is dealing with currency, titles, or other forms of data, this data cannot be altered or changed. All of the blocks of data that have joined the blockchain will be traced back to their original genesis block, so it is easy to trace everything to where it belongs.

The fact that the data is unchangeable and it will help to connect all of the different parts of this blockchain together helps to make a trail that any user can follow if they want to. Most users will not do this, but if they wanted to, it would be easy for them to check out the transactions and make sure that it all fits together.

This security is so important on any network you belong to. Many users are tired of working with financial institutions because there are just too many cases of fraud and manipulation of data that most people have stopped even paying attention. Often, when these cases happen, the rail that would lead back to when the fraud did occur is so altered that it would need a whole investigation to figure out and sometimes this trail has been messed with so much that they will never be able to completely trace back the fraud.

This is not something that happens when you are working on a system with blockchain. Transactions, once they are entered into the database, cannot be altered. This makes sure that all trails on the blockchain are easy to follow. It is possible to make some changes, but the person who did this would need the ability to control over half of the computers on this network at the same time. Since blockchain is used all over the world, this becomes almost impossible. It is not a flawless system, but it is certainly better than the methods we are currently using.

Cons

New technology: While everything about blockchain technology looks good so far, committing to the new standard too soon could easily cause you issues later on. For example, if you compare the bitcoin blockchain

to the Ethereum blockchain then you will notice several instances where the Ethereum
blockchain is superior, including the way in
which it interacts with smart contracts and the
rate at which it can verify transactions. While
the bitcoin blockchain is already reaching its
verification maximum and showing its age, the
Ethereum blockchain is going strong. All this
is to say that becoming too much of an early
adopter can leave you working from a disad-
vantage when the new standard truly takes
over.

This is especially true as only about two percent of all Americans currently interact with a
blockchain on a regular basis. While being on
the forefront of a new technology is always
beneficial, it is important to put blockchain
technology into context before blowing a large
part of your budget on something that is unlikely to gain mainstream acceptance for about
five years. If you need to take some time to
ensure your infrastructure is up to pair to deal
with the blockchain addition, then you certainly have time to do so.

Once data is in, it is in: While the fact that anything that is added to the blockchain is automatically retained and it is generally treated as
a positive, if you are hoping to use your decentralized database to store information that is
going to be altered on a regular basis then it
could likely end up being more trouble than its
worth. In a standard database, changing stored

information is as easy as logging in, making the change, and having the results saved in the log. This is not the case with a blockchain database, however, not by a long shot. Do not forget to change anything that is already a part of the blockchain you are going to need to change it to 51 percent of all nodes, at the same time. While this may be manageable if you need to do it on occasion, making it a regular part of the process is likely to prove more cumbersome than it is worth.

High costs: While there is plenty about blockchain that you should be excited about, the ease with which one can be run and the costs associated with doing so are not on the list. Furthermore, these are not issues that can be combated easily as they are part and parcel of the decentralized nature of the construct. Each node that is created is going to add an additional layer of security to the network, while also adding to the costs of running the decentralized database as a whole. Furthermore, costs will multiply at roughly one to one, regardless of how many nodes you need to set up at once.

This lack of scalability will automatically make a blockchain database a non-starter for a wide variety of companies, especially those who have not yet reached the limits of what their existing system can do. While the costs will vary depending on the needs of the company that is running it, a good benchmark to consider is the cost associated with confirming a single bitcoin transaction. This action which happens thousands of time each day, costs the same amount as powering an average household for 36 hours. While your costs will likely never reach these heights, it goes to show how non-cost effective the technology is.

Pro big business: While blockchain technology can currently be thought of as a fringe technology that has caught on with a certain segment of the investment market, the truth of the matter is that those who ultimately have the most to gain from using the technology are going to be the major corporations. They are the ones with the massive infrastructures in need of an overhaul, and they will see the greatest benefits from decentralization. Every new technology will ultimately rise along with a few companies that serve as the poster child of the minute. The rest of the profits are snatched up by the establishment, and most of the smaller companies will die out.

Those who expect blockchain technology to buck this trend are going to be sadly mistaken. These types of moves are already being made in the industry, and the big fish are already circling the pond with the likes of the Ethereum Enterprise Alliance, among others. While there is nothing inherently wrong with this cycle, it is certainly important to keep it in mind when making your own plans to maximize blockchain's effectiveness in your life.

Creates new security concerns: While those who verify blockchain transactions these days can work in anonymity, this is unlikely to continue as private blockchains become more commonplace. The job of verifying transactions is likely going to become extremely important, and those who do so at the highest levels will likely have security clearance levels to match. This is most certainly going to be required as those with this level of clearance will essentially have free reign to ensure that the system works as intended. The amount of influence these individuals will have will mean that the new security measures will need to be created to keep them in check which means, even more, costs to factor into running a decentralized database.

Limits data mining: This is another factor that consumers are going to be happy about that makes blockchain in its current form difficult for all businesses to get behind. The level of anonymity that is possible when using a blockchain decentralized database makes it difficult to determine the types of interactions that individuals are taking. This in turn, limits the amount of data that corporations can collect on their customers, making the job of their marketing departments more difficult.

As such, if your company is considering moving to a decentralized database, you will need to take into account the extra time that data mining will require along with the additional costs besides. It is also worth keeping in mind that, depending on your desired usage, a blockchain database might simply be a little bit extra security in return for a whole lot more work. It is important to take your specific usage scenario into account before deciding to take the plunge, and only decide to move ahead if there are real benefits to doing so, which might not be the case in every scenario. When deciding to switch to a decentralized database, it is important not just to get caught up in the hype and fully think things through first.

Chapter 5

HOW BLOCKCHAIN CAN RESHAPE FINANCIAL SERVICES

When blockchain was first invented, it was designed to be used with the Bitcoin network. It was designed to help make sure that all transactions on the network would be accounted for and it added some safety and trust to the system. And as Bitcoin started to grow more and it has gained more use around the world, people started to notice the blockchain technology, and they began to imagine some of the other uses that they could do with blockchain.

For those who do not dig in deep enough, the blockchain sometimes looks like a basic accounting tool, something that will hold onto all of the Bitcoin network's transactions, but they did not see it as something that could be expanded out to some other areas. When you start to realize all the things that blockchain can do, many companies are getting excited about how blockchain will be able to help them in the future, and lots of money is going into blockchain right now to help out various industries.

The biggest industry that is using blockchain technology right now is in the finance arena. And since this industry works the same as the transactions on the Bitcoin network, it is really easy to develop some new platforms that will work for the finance industry as well. Block-chain has been shown to process information through the financial industry much faster because it is on a single distributed ledger and it can eliminate the intermediaries so that the process will be faster. This technology can be utilized in many different niches of finance depending on how the platform is developed such as currency transfer, payments, stock trading, and settlements.

The process of transferring any value is a really slow process, especially when you try to compare it to the length of the financial transactions. Depending on the location of the money sent, it can take you a few weeks to move the money. This is really true when you are trying to move money over to other countries and sometimes waiting for the exact exchange rate can be a hassle and will mess with the amount that you pay when it is time to complete the transfer. When you work with the blockchain ledger, you will be able to cut down on the time that it takes to complete these transactions and you can cut down on how much it costs to transfer the value. All of this is so important for helping the financial industry to help their customers.

Not only will this kind of technology be able to help with regular banking methods, but it could also help with share trading. The traditional methods of trading in the stock market will be slow. You need to take your time to look at the stocks, talk with your broker about them, and then before you can make a trade, you will need to make sure that your money can transfer from a bank account over to your trading account. Some people will speed this up and keep a bit of money reserved inside of their trading account, so they do not have to wait when it is time to trade, but there is still some time that you have to worry about. With the help of blockchain, you will be able to speed up the settlement process and can make it easier to get into the trading right when you want to, not when the bank makes it convenient. This technology is so efficient that the NASDAQ has already started to use it with share trading.

The blockchain that NASDAQ is using is the pre-IPO share trades, which makes it easier to transfer share ownership of private companies between the investors before these shares are listed on the stock exchange. This blockchain is already working which shows how easy it would be for other businesses in the finance industry to implement this as well.

There are already some companies who are using this kind of technology to help run their business, not just the NASDAQ. Some of the other options include Visa, Citibank, and Capital One. These three companies are investing in a distributed ledger that will make it easier for them to complete transactions between their institutions, speeding up the process and helping customers get the best service possible.

This is not the only example of the changes that are occurring with the blockchain technology. Ripple is a good example. Ripple is a payment network that is being used to transfer anything of value such as currencies and commodities. Some financial institutions are already investing in and using this kind of technology because it helps them to send out payments at a low cost, and in real time, compared to the other methods that we have been relying on. Right now, there are fifteen of the top banks that are working with Ripple to continue making this kind of platform.

Also, there is a tech firm that is known as R3 that has been working with twenty-five banks, such as Wells Fargo and JP Morgan, to make their own distributed ledger. The companies that have joined this project are a part of the R3 consortium. This is very similar to what is happening with Ripple, but this one is a bit different since it is working with the ledger rather than the exact blockchain technology of Ripple.

The distributed ledger that R3 is developing is a bit different than what the blockchain technology, but they do have some similarities and is offering a lot of the benefits that blockchain already does. Eleven banks that belong to the R3 consortium are already connected to this ledger and are using it to help them provide better customer service.

In England, things are changing up as well. The Bank of England is working to develop their own blockchain technology as well. The Bank of England has decided to change up their own personal database to make it easier to add in this kind of technology to their business plan and they are already teaming up with others to create this technology so that they can serve their customers better in the future. The hope here is that the Bank of England would be able to utilize this technology to help them defend against the many cyber-attacks that are coming to their way and that they would be able to settle up transactions faster. Since many major banks around the world are already implementing blockchain technology and distributed ledgers, The Bank of England is hoping that this system would help them to keep compatible with the other systems as well.

As you can see, there are already many different sectors as well as companies within the finance industry who are working with this kind of technology. There are even some major banks who are working to see if they can add in this technology instead of using their own databases because it can help them save money, complete transactions faster, and provide better service to their customers. While this kind of technology is still in the development phase, there are a lot of potentials and some big companies who are ready to start adopting it once the right platform comes out.

There are many ways that this technology can be used, especially when it comes to the finance industry. Whether they want to speed up the transaction time to customers, save on some of the costs of their ledgers, or they want to make sure they are changing the future of technology, there are many reasons that people will choose to go with this new kind of technology.

Chapter 6

THE TECHNOLOGY BEHIND BITCOIN AND CRYPTOCURRENCY

There are quite a few applications for block-chain platforms, which we did discuss earlier, but it was a technology that was designed to work with the Bitcoin network to make sure that this network would be transparent but still allow for the security that people were looking for. Because of all this, it is common for people to assume that blockchain and cryp-tocurrencies are the same.

There are some big differences between the two, and they are not the same. To start, Bitcoin is a type of digital currency that you can use to make purchases and send money all around the world. You can choose to join in the Bitcoin network, or with one of the other digital currencies, and then you would use those coins to make purchases and so on. This is a currency that is only found online, so you will never be able to print the currency and use it at your favorite stores that you can with tra-ditional money. But many find this as a benefit because they can just find the stores they want to use online and then make their purchases.

There are quite a few benefits that come with using Bitcoin. You can make sure that the gov-ernment stays out of your transactions, you can save money with the international trade because you will not need to deal with expensive intermediaries, and you will be amazed at how quickly these transactions can be finished.

The blockchain is a bit different, and it is described as a distributed ledger. It is in charge of keeping track of all sorts of transactions, and it can be set up to hold onto anything that is considered valuable. When someone enters new information into the blockchain, it is really hard to change this information later; you can only change the information if you get control of over half the computers on the network. This will make sure that the network is safe and that no one can go through and make changes to the transactions that are found on the blockchain.

Now, these two technologies can help out each other, and in fact, blockchain was released at the same time as Bitcoin to help this currency run. Since there is not a big bank or other government agency around to run the country, Bitcoin, as well as some of the other digital currencies that are out there, needed to have something in place that would build up the trust that users needed. Without blockchain being around, it would be hard to convince people that their transactions are safe and they would not be likely to use the system at all.

While these two are different types of technologies, it is unlikely that digital currencies would be as successful as they are today if blockchain was not around to help things out. Many people would choose to not go with these because they wanted to make sure that their money was as safe as possible. Block-chain adds that element of trust without people having to worry about whether someone can see his or her information, whether he or she needs that third party to help out, or something else.

Does blockchain really help digital currencies?

The big question now is how blockchain really works to help make these digital currencies successful. To understand how this happens, we will first need to take some time to look at how blockchain runs We talked about this a bit earlier in the guide, but there is a lot more that comes into play so let's take a look.

To review, a blockchain is basically going to be a database that can hold onto all of the transactions that occur on the Bitcoin network. The full copy of the blockchain, such as the one that you will find on the Bitcoin network, is going to contain each transaction that has ever occurred on the network since it started. With this information, it is possible for any users that would like to, to find out information on the transactions that go on within the network.

Now, this system is also set up to add in some security so that people can keep their information as safe as possible. Every block will be given a hash that is unique but which is still based on some of the information from the previous block (the miners are going to be responsible for this kind of work). This will end up creating a big chain of blocks that are meant to connect together in perfect order from start to finish. Through this particular method, each block is going to be in the right order, or there would be some issues with the hashes present.

Once a new block is added into the blockchain, it is then impossible to make any modifications to the transactions in that block. To try and make changes would mean that the hash for each block that came after it would have to be changed as well and this would result in a big mess. This is how things are supposed to be though. The creators came up with this system because they do not want to allow someone to enter the network and make changes without being quite noticeable.

Honest generators, who are known as the miners, will only be able to build on a new block if it is the newest block on the longest valid chain. The length is going to be calculated as a total to the combined difficulty in that chain, rather than how many blocks, although this distinction is not really that important except for a few types of attacks. A chain will be considered valid if all the transactions and the blocks that are found inside of it are valid, and only if there is the right genesis block in place.

If this process has gone smoothly with no issues along the way, all the blocks will lead all the way back to the genesis block without any issues. However, it is possible for this genesis block to have some forks inside of it, so there can be different directions. One-block forks are created when two blocks have been developed at the same time. If this does happen, the generating nodes will work to build on the block that they received first. And then there are times when a bigger fork will show up because the program was working to fix some bugs in the system.

Blocks that are near the end of some of the longer chains can be added to the main part because they do add some more value. However, if we are dealing with some blocks that are on shorter trains, which are sometimes called invalid chains, they are going to be left alone and not used. If the user of Bitcoin switches over to one of the longer chains, all of the ones on that shorter chain can then be queued so that they can be added in as well.

As this illustrates, there are quite a few ways that this amazing technology can benefit the users of digital currencies. This process is complex, but it shows what is going on each time you complete a transaction on the Bitcoin network, and it will help to keep your information safe and secure, which is why Bitcoin really needs the platform to work well.

Now, you may be wondering how you would get one of these blocks to get started and to keep your information secure. When you decide to join the Bitcoin network, you will receive your own unique address and an invitation to the network. Then that first block is going to be sent to you automatically. Depending on how many transactions that you complete, you will be able to fill up that block over so much time. Each block can hold onto a certain amount of transactions, and sometimes this will take a while based on how busy you are on the network.

After the block has some time to fill up, it will be time for that block to become a part of the permanent record and join the rest of the chain. Your chain may be long if you do many transactions on this network, but it could also be a bit smaller if you only get on the Bitcoin network on occasion. Over time, as they join the permanent record, these personal chains will be added into the big blockchains so that everything remains safe.

As we mentioned, this is where the miners are going to need to get to the work. They are in charge of creating some unique codes, or hashes, that will help hide the personal information inside of the blocks, while still keeping the information transparent. The new blocks will have hashes that link them back to the block in front of it and so on down the line. There are also some other requirements that are in place for creating these hashes, which will help to make sure that no one can mess with the system.

When the miners are successful for the work that they are doing, they will be rewarded with 25 Bitcoin. With how high the value of Bitcoin is today, this can be a good reward for helping to keep the whole network safe. The miners will receive a monetary reward for their work, and all of the Bitcoin users will know that their information is safe.

When the block has been given a new hash, it will then be sent on to join the main block-chain, and it will then be a part of the perma-nent records.

Users can then check out all of the information that is there and make sure that all transac-tions are in the right place at the right time whenever they would want. Thanks to the work of the miners, and the basics of the blockchain system, your information is always going to be safe when using Bitcoin.

Blockchain has really made a difference in how Bitcoin and other digital currencies work. Blockchain has a lot of different applications, and it is already being developed to use in various industries throughout the world, but without it, Bitcoin would end up failing because it would not have a way to build up trust with the users.

Chapter 7

7 KILLER BLOCKCHAIN APPLICATIONS THAT ARE SHAPING OUR FUTURE

Distributed Cloud Storage

Several companies, including Storj (pronounced storage) Labs, have already started taking advantage of blockchain technology to offer cloud storage services. Their app makes use of blockchain's inherent security features to ensure your files remain secure while they are in the cloud. Storj is an open source project that is taking advantage of consumer demand for this type of service in order to crowdsource a majority of the work on its service by an ever-growing community of developers.

Storj's application works by first organizing a group of individuals who are interested in renting out space on their hard drives and also have the extra bandwidth they are not using. It then connects these individuals via a peer to peer network which Storj claims is not only faster but also cheaper than larger cloud-based storage solutions.

The way large companies offer these types of services involves massive data centers that serve as the hub for all of these cloud storage services. These data centers naturally are quite cost prohibitive to build, and the price for running so many servers means the price does not decrease much once things are up and running. Not only does this type of scenario mean higher costs that are then passed on to the consumer, but it also makes it easier for hackers to attack the data because it is all centrally located.

Storj, and other companies like it, face none of these problems as their decentralized nature naturally neutralizes all of the issues that these companies face. Currently, Storj boasts more than 15,000 users taking advantage of the hard drive space of more than 7,500 computers.

Digital Identity

IBM has partnered with a company named SecureKey Technologies to work on an initiative designed to promote the usage of digital identities on a global scale. It can connect government agencies, healthcare providers, telcos and banks through a single, shared blockchain network. This network runs on an IBM blockchain that will utilize the Hyperledger technology created by the Linux Foundation.

It utilizes a distributed trust model that will allow users to control the details that are shared, as well as which organizations have access to it and even ensure they are allowed to give their consent before their information is accessed in the first place.

The system has already caught on in Canada with some major banks including the Bank of Montreal, TD Bank, Scotiabank, Royal Bank of Canada, Desjardins Group and Canadian Imperial Bank of Commerce has already jumped on board. The system is set up in such a way that it is easily scalable for new members who can get started with a minimal extra effort from an operational standpoint. As with private cloud storage, the benefits of blockchain's natural security shine through here, though the distributed ledger is obviously also quite critical, especially for the financial sector.

Smart Contracts

While smart contracts have the potential to revolutionize a great deal of the day to day world, as of 2017, they are primarily being used on the Ethereum Blockchain platform. The Ethereum blockchain was created to interface with smart contracts as effectively as possible, and there are already numerous different decentralized applications that are running on its system.

Smart contracts are currently being used for a wide variety of purpose on the platform including for things like facilitating contract negations. Smart contracts are also seeing use when it comes to insurance policies. This can dramatically shorten the period of time that is required to process a claim and will continue to shorten it even more as internet-enabled vehicles to become more and more prevalent. In these instances, the insurance company writes the smart contract into the policy and then when specific input conditions are met that are within the range of insured events, the client would be paid out automatically.

Smart contracts are also making great strides when it comes to the way that copyrighted content is handled. The company Blockphase has already released a tool to help content creators who work in the 360-degree, augmented reality and virtual reality space a new option when it comes to ensuring their content is secured online. Content that is uploaded to the Blockphase blockchain is then automatically searched for on a regular basis, and if finds a match, it reaches out to the user to request payment. The end result is that artists can focus more on content creation and less on the business side of things.

In the digital media space, the company ContentKid is working to change the way that content subscriptions are handled. The way it works is that users with accounts to subscription content sign up and rent out portions of their service to those who are interested in just watching a single show. The payment for doing so is made via a smart contract in ContentKid's blockchain, and all the login functionality is as well to ensure that user credentials are not available where they should not be.

Decentralized Notary

As previously discussed, many of the core facets of blockchain technology naturally lend themselves to the unique requirements of notary services. Companies, such as Stamped.io, have been quick to notice and capitalize on this fact and there are now several different applications that allow you to access notary services without going to hassle of performing the task the old-fashioned way. In countries like India, a reduction in the headaches related to these services will represent a serious step forward as the current process is extremely long and arduous. It will also represent a huge asset in countries where services like these are extremely rare or irregular.

Apps such as Stamped take advantage of the blockchain of the users choosing to verify the authenticity of the file, directly from a browser window. Once a document has been uploaded, the document is then applied a digital timestamp, and its certification is handled via a SHA256 hash on the blockchain in question. The process can be applied to any type of file and can be used to certify that it was in the owner's possession at the specific point in time.

Digital Voting

When it comes to improving the voting process, blockchain is a natural means of doing so as any votes cast will naturally be easily verifiable and secure, they will also be very easy to count which means there will be no worries when it comes to knowing exactly who won what. The online platform Follow My Vote is currently working to create just this type of online voting service in the name of improving transparency in elections of all types. This type of system is likely to greatly increase voter turnout while also reducing the overall cost and increasing the efficiency of elections that do occur.

The app works with specialized voting booths that record each user's government ID and then add that voter's information to the Follow My Vote blockchain. After the fact, they can then use the voter ID number that they were issued to go back in and ensure that their vote was counted correctly. Furthermore, this process allows voters to watch the election progress in real time while the votes are being cast.

The system even allows voters to go back in and change their votes if they change their minds before the election is over.

Networking and IoT

IBM makes it on the list again due to its work with blockchain and the internet of things. The internet of things allows a wide variety of internet-connected devices to communicate with one another for a wide variety of purposes. The Watson IoT platform is a scalable platform that was created to serve as a centralized hub for all the IoT needs of a modern business. The system also offers machine learning, image and text analytics and natural language processing to make fulfilling the needs of the company as easy as possible.

This technology is having a transformative effect on a wide variety of industries, including the automotive industry where the cognitive effect of the internet of things is already working to bring self-driving cars to the market. Over 60 percent of all automotive manufacturers are currently considering ways to which they can add this technology to their products.

Payment and Money Transfers

While blockchain and Ethereum are the first names that come to mind when it comes to blockchain based money transfer and payment system, there are plenty of other alternatives out there. One such application is Ripple which provides a blockchain based payment network that is already connecting corporations, digital asset exchanges, payment providers and banks together to help users transfer money all around the world. Ripple is already working with more than 90 banks from all around the world.

Ripple's service works from a three-pronged approach; banks utilize a service known as xCurrent to process payments on a global scale for their customers. Payment providers then use a service called xRapid to find liquidity on demand from around the world and businesses can use the xVia service to send payments directly through Ripple's blockchain. Ripple uses its own cryptocurrency, called XRP that can already be purchased through a wide variety of different cryptocurrency exchanges around the world.

Chapter 8

THE TECHNICAL GUIDE TO THE BLOCKCHAIN TECHNOLOGY

Database differences

When compared to a more traditional database, a decentralized database such as blockchain, the biggest difference is their primary goal. A centralized database is all about ensuring that users can access its data as quickly as possible. A decentralized database on the other hand, gives up on the idea of speed entirely in exchange for allowing users to access the database from literally anywhere in the entire world. When combined with the security features of the blockchain that were discussed in previous chapters, along with its innate ability to accurately sort vast amounts of data means it offers up database storage that is both autonomous and secure.

Hashes

Data that is stored in the blockchain can be broken down into details about the block itself and the details regarding any relevant transactions the block might hold. While the data about the block itself is only going to make up a small portion of the block as a whole, it is still exceedingly detailed. Once the information inside the block is verified, the block is encrypted via what is known as a hash function. Once this is done, even if a hacker managed to break into the data stream of a blockchain, they would not be able to access complete transaction records and instead would be faced with a fixed length output which is the digital fingerprint of the data in question.

Changing even a single digit of this resulting code would alter the data in unpredictable ways. The hash function that a majority of blockchains use is SHA-256. Data that is encrypted in this fashion can only be decoded via a special hash key. Each block receives a base hash once it has been added to the chain, and then all of its individual transactions receive unique hashes as well. The block's hashes are then modified even more based on its location in the chain and the blocks that are directly around it. If the details of a block do not match the details of the blocks around it, then it will be removed from the chain.

Merkle Root

The Merkle process makes it much easier for blockchains to work in a manner that is as efficient as possible, while still maintaining their high level of accuracy. Known as a Merkle tree or Merkle root, this process can be thought of as a functionality matrix that maximizes efficiency. They also make it easier for financial transactions to be compacted in such a way that they can be broken down into digestible portions so that users can more easily process the continuous flow of data.

While it is possible to build a blockchain without the Merkle process, doing so only results in blockchain that is slower and overall more difficult to use. Each time a new block is added to the chain, its hash is combined with the hashes of those that came before it and so on and so forth up the line until the entire blockchain has a unique hash called the hash root that changes with each new block that is added to it. This hash root can be thought of as the total of all of the information that is currently stored in the chain. The root hash can then be easily used to secure the blockchain and make it easy for the system to determine if any of its blocks have been altered.

Rather than having to check all of the information in all of the blocks, the Merkle tree just has to check each hash, and as long as they all match up, then the blockchain is secure. Merkle trees received their name based on the way in which they process information by creating branches at every point. One branch sees the information in question as correct; the other does not. Both outcomes exist simultaneously until the information is verified in one way or the other. This way, when a block is flagged as troublesome, the Merkle tree can protect the sanctity of the blockchain while at the same time not letting block exist if it is not accurate.

Checking the amount of data contained in a blockchain for accuracy manually would be an almost impossible task that would make the verification process even more cumbersome than it already is. The Merkle tree simplifies this process and also limits the amount of data that is required to be shared between nodes. This in turn, makes it a comparatively simpler process of determining when there is a disparity between a pair of disparate nodes, while also making it easier to determine what is the correct information in a given situation.

Each time a hash is flagged as potentially incorrect, it is flagged while the next succession of branches continues being checked. This makes the process much faster than it would otherwise be if the data in every node needed to be checked before the next could be. This is when the hashes are verified for accuracy, and any required changes to the database are made.

For a Merkle tree to run as efficiently as possible, it is important that a certain degree of trust regarding the system is maintained. Specifically, the user must trust in the absolute inviolability of the blockchain, and thus its continued viability. This means that if a user decides to download the latest node software, then they will be able to trust in the fact that it is the most accurate version of the blockchain currently available. Additionally, there needs the trust that if any nefarious nodes are created, they will be weeded out through the security process and that the blocks it creates will have hashes that do not match the way they should. If multiple nodes provide the same inaccurate information, then that information is thrown out, and the last verifiable, accurate information is used instead.

A closer look at smart contracts

Smart contracts, as previously mentioned are a type of code that interacts with a blockchain to activate a wide variety of yes or no variables. The Ethereum platform has seen great improvements in the utilization of smart contracts and is currently considered the hands-down leader in the space. The Ethereum platform allows anyone to create decentralized applications that can be run on its service in exchange for gas, or service fees paid out in the ether. We will discuss more about the smart contracts in the next chapter.

Chapter 9

SMART CONTRACTS

From the first introduction of Bitcoin, crypto-currency has been going through a major evolution with an endless stream of improvements with each new emerging currency. Smart contracts are just one of those evolutionary changes in a digital currency that has lots of advantages.

What Is a Smart Contract?

The term "smart contract" has no clear and settled definition.

The idea has long been hyped to the public as a central component of next-generation blockchain platforms, and as a key capability for any practical enterprise application.

They are defined variously as "autonomous machines," "contracts between parties stored on a blockchain" or "any computation that takes place on a blockchain." Many debates about the nature of smart contracts are really just contests between competing terminologies. The best way to describe smart contracts is to compare the technology to a vending machine. Ordinarily, you would go to a lawyer or a notary, pay them, and wait while you get the document. With smart contracts, you simply drop a bitcoin into the vending machine (i.e., ledger), and your escrow, driver's license, or whatever drops into your account. More so, smart contracts not only define the rules and penalties around an agreement in the same way that a traditional contract does, but also automatically enforce those obligations.

Another way to understanding smart contracts is to realize that these are digital versions of real contracts. With a standard contract between two parties, you have an agreement that stipulates what each party must do for the transaction to be completed. The contract actually sets the parameters of who does what, when to do it, how to do it, and what happens once it's been done.

Up until Smart Contracts, these agreements have only been in verbal or written form subjected to territorial laws and regulations of the land where they were drawn up. Also, with these contracts, the terms of the contract could always subject to interpretation.

Today's Smart Contracts improve on all of that. Firstly, these digital agreements are designed to be self-executing and enforced without any additional party to weigh in on the matter. There is no need to have the language of the agreement interpreted in any way.

Rather than writing them in spoken language, Smart Contracts are written in computer code and programming languages that stipulate the terms and expectations of the agreement.

There are many advantages to this form of coded contracts that you may not readily recognize. These contracts do not need a company or regulations to enforce them. This means that there is no longer a bureaucracy or any associated costs for such services. They can actually be something like a do-it-yourself contract allowing them to self-manage based on the terms agreed upon by only the parties involved. Basically, you could look at them as programmable money, allowing users to solve common problems themselves.

Several cryptocurrencies are already using smart contracts including Bitcoin, Ethereum, and Lisk. However, this is only the beginning. Smart contracts are so efficient and practical that more currencies will be adopting them as the world of cryptocurrency continues to grow and expand.

How You Can Use Smart Contracts

Jerry Cuomo, vice president for blockchain technologies at IBM, believes smart contracts can be used all across the chain from financial services to healthcare to insurance. Here are some examples:

Government

Insiders vouch that it is extremely hard for our

voting system to be rigged, but nonetheless, smart contracts would allay all concerns by providing an infinitely more secure system. Ledger-protected votes would need to be decoded and require excessive computing power to access.

No one has that much computing power, so it would need God to hack the system! Secondly, smart contracts could hike low voter turnout. Much of the inertia comes from a fumbling system that includes lining up, showing your identity, and completing forms. With smart contracts, volunteers can transfer voting online, and millennials will turn out en masse to vote for their Potus.

Management

The blockchain not only provides a single ledger as a source of trust, but also shaves possible snarls in communication and workflow because of its accuracy, transparency, and automated system. Ordinarily, business operations have to endure a back-and-forth, while waiting for approvals and for internal or external issues to sort themselves out.

A blockchain ledger streamlines this. It also cuts out discrepancies that typically occur with independent processing, and that may lead to costly lawsuits and settlement delays.

Automobile

There's no doubt that we're progressing from slothful pre-human vertebrates to super-smart robots. Think of a future where everything is automated. Google's getting there with smartphones, smart glasses, and even smart cars. That's where smart contracts help. One example is the self-autonomous or self-parking vehicles, where smart contracts could put into play a sort of 'oracle' that could detect who was at fault in a crash; the sensor or the driver, as well as countless other variables. Using smart contracts, an automobile insurance company could charge rates differently based on where, and under which conditions customers are operating their vehicles.

Chapter 10

BUSINESS IN THE ERA OF BLOCKCHAIN

Improved operations

Businesses have long been stymied by the banking establishment as this required intermediary which has not only proven itself to be untrustworthy from time to time but the costs required to do business are clearly not doing business owners any favors. On the contrary, regardless of the blockchain you choose to handle your business on, you are likely to find more reasonable fees, access to money operations in real time, and the security that most banks can only dream about. Furthermore, using this technology makes it easier for companies to expand their focus to global lengths as transactions made in this way are not restricted in any of the ways that the traditional banking establishment limits things.

Distributed ledger

When it comes to small businesses, the biggest benefit of blockchain technology is its distributed ledger aspect. The dataset that are part of it is not owned by a middleman or any third party and is instead freely available across the network where every interested party can easily verify their own version of the ledger based on their own copy. What's more, each user will remain fully in control of all of their information and transaction details which means there will be no central point of failure where cyber-attacks are more likely to occur.

This technology provides such a security boon to businesses that a representative from Nasdaq even weighed in on the issue saying that even if a hacker were able to penetrate the blockchain's security measures, there would still be multiple redundant copies of the same file, one for every node, so restoring funds to their proper place is a simple matter of redistributing data where it needs to be. Forbes also chimed in on the topic praising blockchain technology for its built-in trust mechanisms that small businesses should be in a rush to adopt.

When transactions are processed via a blockchain, the fee that is charged goes in part to the owner of the blockchain to offset costs, and the rest goes to the miners who ultimately verify the transaction. Despite having to pay out two parties, blockchain fees are significantly less than business frequently pay for similar services through traditional financial institutions. When the number of transactions that the average business completes in a month is taken into account, the savings that blockchain offers can be truly significant.

Ease of use

Another important benefit that small business owners are sure to appreciate when it comes to blockchain technology is the amount it will help to streamline common business practices. The process of settling or clearing bank transactions can easily take days via traditional methods. Not so with blockchain on the task, however, as the verification process of even the slowest blockchain is going to beat traditional banking speeds with ease, especially for transactions that are conducted over the weekend.

When smart contract technology is added into the equation, the potential for streamlining and automation of all types becomes much more manageable. While some of the more advanced methods of taking advantage of blockchain technology are likely going to be too pricey for some small businesses to take advantage of, the cost of such endeavors will continue to decrease as the tasks that are required to complete them become more mundane. All told, the technology is sure to make any organization run more efficiently while also cutting the costs.

Improved contracts

Business is inherently about transferring value between various parties. Blockchain provides the most secure environment currently conceivable and even provides the means in the form of smart contracts. Any contract that includes numerous if-then statements can easily be carried out via smart contract which will not only ensure the transactions in question that are carried out; it will also improve trust between business associates because everyone will be able to watch the transaction of terms take place in real time. By combining contracts with code, smart contracts provide a service that is both free of risk and utterly revolutionary to the way that relationships between businesses and their subcontractors and vendors handle business.

Smart contracts are also useful in that they cut down on the need for corporate bloat, as they eliminate the need for lawyers in most cases. Even better, they also eliminate the need for pricey legal proceedings that may result in one party not sticking to the agreement. If smart contracts have been activated, there is no chance that the agreed-upon transaction will not go through as long as all the agreed upon variables have been met. With the contract on the blockchain, the possibility of either party successfully changing the agreement once it has been struck to zero.

Logistical piece of mind

Companies that deal with a large degree of logistical and shipping data should be extremely interested in blockchain technology for the easy and transparency it can potentially bring into their lives. Most systems make it difficult to determine the exact location of specific goods and shipments when real-time updates are needed. This then leads to delays which can negatively affect the business in a wide variety of ways and, at the best result in additional costs and a strain on customers and vendors.

Proof of provenance is another pressing issue as in a majority of instances the product that eventually reaches the consumer was not created by just one manufacturer. As an example, consider a furniture company that sources wood from China and fittings from Italy who in turn source their base materials from somewhere in Eastern Europe. Tracking all of the various components from doorstep to doorstep is practically impossible using current methods; however, using a blockchain tracking system, it then becomes easy to determine if the wood was generated due to illegal logging practices or if the fittings are made from metal with hazardous properties. What's more, blockchain makes all these specific details easy to find and track with practically no effort on the part of the company.

As the infrastructure for the internet of things improves, it will eventually become possible to track absolutely every step in the process of every product. Eventually, even consumers will be able to track the path their products took from the factory floor to their very doorstep, with just a few clicks of a button.

Cheaper storage

Businesses spend more than $20 billion every single year on cloud storage solutions, despite the fact that a majority of existing data storage space remains unused. What's worse, as a company with higher than average data needs, you need to entrust your most pertinent data to a third party if you hope to successfully store it in the long-term. Cloud storage options based on blockchain technology will not only ensure that your most important data remains safe and secure exactly where you left it, but it will also decrease costs significantly as well. In fact, for companies who are only looking into blockchain technology for storage purposes, a cloud-based storage option will likely cost about a tenth of what creating and operating a full blockchain would probably cost.

Smart offices

The future is going to be full of sensors. Each day more and more offices are being connected to digital assistants, and this trend towards interconnectivity is only going to continue to grow. As with logistical technology, the continued growth of the internet of things means that offices are going to become more and more interconnected as time goes on. Once autonomous office networks go online, all of the office equipment will be able to communicate with one another and will gain the ability to self-manage, schedule and pay for maintenance via blockchain technology, auto-update, fix bugs and more. Blockchain technology will also allow for the automatic purchase of consumables such as printer ink or paper when one or the other runs low.

Not only would office equipment take such things itself saving time, but it will also save money in several different ways as well. Certain functions can automatically be scheduled during periods outside of peak usage hours, and the equipment will only use exactly as much energy it needs to get things done. It will also prevent a buildup of unnecessary supplies and ensure that no productivity is lost when waiting for key components to arrive. While letting your office manage itself might seem like mainly a novelty, it has the potential to seriously cut into your expenses in the long run.

Looking forward

Overall, it is hard to say just how blockchain technology is going to benefit small businesses moving forward, though it is already benefiting major corporations in a variety of ways today. Regardless of the size of your business, if you are interested in becoming more connected via blockchain technology, then the first thing you are going to need to do is to ensure you approach the entire endeavor in a cool, calm manner. Having your mind made up in one direction or another, right from the start, is no way to ensure you reliably make a good decision. When approaching blockchain opportunities, it is important to keep in mind that the technology is still very new and nothing about it has yet been set in stone.

Chapter 11

EXECUTIVE'S GUIDE TO IMPLEMENTING BLOCKCHAIN TECHNOLOGY

Internal strategies for tackling blockchain

When it comes to implementing blockchain technology successfully, it is important to keep in mind that your efforts to do so will always be more effective if you focus on using it in such a way that it makes the most of your company's unique strengths. As an example, a company that is known to be extremely responsive when it comes to customer service, as well as their rapid fulfillment of orders, could then take advantage of what blockchain technology can do for logistics to improve their speeds even further and ensure they stay one step ahead of the market.

Nevertheless, when moving forward, it is important to keep in mind that the technology is still far too new to base your entire company on. As such, your best bet is going to be an investment that allows your company to explore this new technology in a strategic way to minimize costs before you know exactly what the benefits will be. The best way to go about doing so is to create a core technology working group to look into the best way of implementing this basic technology.

It is important to keep a close eye on them, however, as groups like these can get caught up in the unmitigated potential of the new technology and focus so much on implementation that they forget to focus on core strengths. To prevent this from occurring it is important that they have someone advocating for the importance of sticking to your company's strategic goals and focus on utilizing blockchain in a way that makes the most of its unique value proposition. This person should be from middle management and is typically referred to as the blockchain czar; this person will be responsible for shaping the discussing on blockchain both at the working group level and when it is discussed more officially at higher levels as well.

Planning out the future: The first thing the working group is going to need to do is to find the best opportunities to implement blockchain in the company, thus charting the course moving forward. The first thing they will need to do is to create a list of pilot projects where utilizing blockchain technology will make a measurable difference. When making this list, the first place you are going to start is with the company's traditional pain points including common client complaints, routine delays, and commonly used workarounds.

The decisions that the working group makes at this stage should not be made in a vacuum, and it is important that they get out among the specialists and shareholders from within and without the organization to ensure they are viewing all possible alternatives. The group may naturally skew towards options that are linked to the greatest amount of disruption or the latest trends, but it will be up to the blockchain czar to preach temperance and remind everyone that true change often happens slower than the adoption rate as discussed in the media.

Instead, it is important to choose starting projects that are going to do the most to improve the capabilities of the company in the overall shortest period of time. Focuses on ways that will help the company outpace the competition will generate proof that blockchain technology is worth pursuing and will help generate support for secondary projects that may be less flashy.

Make the required preparations: Once the working group has created a list of potential starting points, the next thing they are going to need to do is to create some specific hypotheses that describe exactly how the blockchain technology will actually make a difference. As an example, the hypothesis could be blockchain technology that will decrease the time required for adjustments as well the need for them in the first place while also increasing transparency. This could be tested by using Ripple or another similar setup to manage the movement of money internally throughout the company.

Solidifying these hypotheses will require another round of consultation with primary business stakeholders in addition to key customer groups, functional teams, and internal business groups. They should also make contact with the financial team, IT, operations, compliance, regulatory committees and risk assessment among others. While this will certainly make getting any initial project off the ground quite a chore, it will be more effective to get all the required input now, rather than having to go back and start over later due to an easily fixable issue.

Put thoughts into action: Once the team has solidified their hypotheses, the next thing they will need to do is to put their prototypes into play. When it comes to implementation, they will then adjust the parameters until the prototypes are working as effectively as possible. During the evaluation and testing phase, the team is sure to improve common practices and also determine new and unexpected ways to put the blockchain technology to work as effectively as possible.

During this phase, it is possible that the prototypes will become so altered that they no longer remain true to the primary hypothesis. To ensure that this is not the case it is the blockchain czar's job to ensure that the end result will still be relevant to the core strengths of the company and the capabilities that the team set out to improve upon in the first place. The czar will also need to monitor momentum during this phase carefully and ensure the team is hitting their milestones. If they are not, it is the czar's job to find out why.

When testing it is important to ensure that the team is testing from a fair place. Those in charge should not be beholden to one result, or the other and prototype leaders should be naturally skeptical while still having a firm understanding of the technology in play. The timeframe for development should be long enough that the team will be able to get to the true heart of the matter, but not so long that they have no motivation to finish as quickly as possible.

Scale up: Once the prototypes are operating properly, all that is left to determine the true cost of implementation on a large scale and work out a timeframe for doing, so that is realistic based on the challenges that it requires. Before making the changes that the team recommends, it is important to focus once more on the core of your business and ask how this will impact it for the better. Make sure to answer the question of how it will change the way the company does business with its primary vendors or customers.

Additionally, it is important to keep in mind that the full-scale implementation of blockchain technology is often a long-term proposition. When it comes to setting the goals for the project, it is important to start with just a few long-range goals for the new technology, quality improvements, cost reductions, improved compliance and the like, and then get buy-in on them from all the relevant parties. A unified approach will make it easier to create an implementation and scaling roadmap that actually has a chance of being followed.

Your roadmap should include how the company will be affected by the new technology, how long it will take to implement and how much it will cost compared to how much it will save or earn in the long run. If the roadmap does not make fiscal sense, then you limited your investment to the prototypes and can easily write it off; on the other hand, if it works out, then you know exactly what to expect from the end results.

Creating decentralized applications

If you plan on creating your own app, then the Ethereum platform is the best one to jump in. The Ethereum platform has quickly proven itself to be the premier destination for those who are looking to utilize decentralized apps for a wide variety of smart contract-based services. To create an app that your company can use, you are going to want to utilize the Solidity programing language which takes advantage of the .sol as well as the .se extension and as well the Lisk byproduct LLL. All of this is sure to feel familiar to any programmer that has previous experience with either Serpent or Python.

For compilation purposes, you are going to need a C++ compatible solc complier. Likewise, you will also ensure that you have access to the Web3.ja API after you have finished compiling your work to ensure that your app can take advantage of the required JavaScript code that will connect the smart contract to the app directly. This is a crucial step when it comes to convenience as it will allow users to access the app without having to first log into an Ethereum node directly.

To get started as quickly as possible, you will go ahead and choose an existing distributed application framework as opposed to going through the trouble of building one from the ground up. The Ethereum community is full of extremely competent developers who want nothing more than to see the platform succeed and they have released a wide variety of different frameworks to ensure there is something readily available that meets the needs of any business.

If you are interested in ensuring your blockchain has access to the best stack possible, you may want to consider the Meteor framework which is also known to work natively with the Web3.js API which makes it the first choice of many developers currently working in the space. Its community is also known to be one of the biggest supporters of the platform overall.

It will also be beneficial to pick up Truffle and Embark which both aim to streamline the app production process, Truffle is perfect for companies that are just getting into the blockchain business as it automates several parts of the programming process which means programmers will have more time to fine-tune the code they are creating as opposed to going over a series of route steps type and again. Embark, then proves itself to be exceedingly useful when it comes to automating the testing process to keep the flow of the project moving as smoothly as possible.

The API that you are going to run across most frequently can be found at BlockApps.net. It is extremely useful as it acts as an Ethereum node if you are not near one when you need to interact with your app. Another variation on the same service is known as MetaMask which runs an Ethereum node out of any web browser. If your company's plan calls for a wide variety of different user types, then you will have to consider LightWallet which allows programmers to easily create decentralized apps that utilize different interfaces for various user groups.

App creation

To create a decentralized app successfully, the first thing you are going to need to do is to generate an Ethereum node to work with. You can go about doing so through the Ethereum interface which is known as Geth. Geth can be downloaded from Install-Geth.ethereum.org. After you have downloaded and installed the program, you will then be able to access the programming environment by opening the console. To quit the console, all you will need to do is to hit "enter." If this occurs, then the console will automatically log what you were working which will be accessible at a later date with the tail-fgeth.log command.

With this done, you will then be free to create the application or smart contract of your dreams, if you can conceive of it, then odds are you can program it, the window of things that are unachievable with blockchain is shrinking every day. Once you have finished with the code, the next thing you will need to do is compile your workings using the solc C++ compiler. After everything has been compiled successfully, you will then be able to deploy the results. This will require the payment of a gas fee in ether and also a digital signature as well.

With this out of the way, you will then receive an email that contains the address of the app or smart contract in the blockchain along with an ABI as well. After the ABI is received, you will then be able to access to what you have created from anywhere, not just the Ethereum node. Depending on the purpose of your creation, it may require gas to power on a regular basis or it may not.

If your goal was to create a smart contract, then it is crucial that your if-then statements are all on point. To ensure that this is the case it is recommended that you use Truffle to generate the basic framework that you are looking to create and then just fill in the specifics. After you have finished with testing, the contract can then be deployed via Truffle directly. This can be done from the console through the truffle init command to generate a new primary directory. It is always important to test compile before you compile to ensure everything will proceed smoothly when it counts.

With this done, you will then need to find the contract you have created and add it to the space saved for contracts in the app.json/config folder. With this done, you can then open your Ethereum node and using the command tesrpc. You will then need to launch Truffle once more before selecting the option to deploy via the root directory.

Chapter 12

7 INDUSTRIES THAT BLOCKCHAIN WILL DISRUPT IN THE FUTURE

Private Transport and Ride Sharing

With the ever-increasing prevalence of ride sharing a private transport option, it is only a matter of time before blockchain technology is put to use in a sector that already heavily relies on automation and ease of use. The private transport industry is likely to see significant changes in a few primary ways, the first of which is through the development of specialized ride sharing blockchains. With a blockchain and specific cryptocurrency dedicated to private transportation, the technology will give rise to specialized wallets where funds for transportation are automatically deducted after rides are concluded, and new funds are added from primary accounts without any effort added on the part of the user.

The increased ease of use that these services would add to the already simple ride sharing experience means that the proliferation of these services is going to continue to increase at a rapid pace. Rather than be owned by a private company, such as Uber or Lyft, these services are likely going to be as decentralized as the technology they use to exist in the first place. Anyone will be able to jump in and provide rides at any time, with no centralized authority holding the ship together.

A variation of this system is already being created while allowing car owners to fund a wallet to automatically pay for fuel, be it electricity or gasoline, as well as for things like parking and toll lanes. If their driving earns them a ticket, the fee for that can also be automatically deducted from the account as well.

Cyber Security

Cybersecurity is a topic that is hugely important across the globe and at all levels of security clearance so much that the World Economic Forum currently considers it as one of the most serious threats facing the world today. Blockchain offers a wide variety of security bonuses which means it is likely to start showing up more and more frequently in discussions about the topic across the globe.

While blockchain's natural security features can be used to beef up a variety of security systems without any additional help, the potential biggest boon for cybersecurity is sure to come in the way that could potentially be used to rebuild the internet from the ground up. Blockchain's decentralized nature could easily be put to work in such a way that it could help to mitigate distributed denial of service attacks. If the new internet properly took advantage of the distributed nature of the blockchain database, it could even remove the possibility of these types of attacks from the internet completely.

It could also be used to manage how an individual's information is distributed online. With the right set of standards in place, users could control how their information is used completely, using a cryptographic key to log in once and have all of their relevant information stored automatically. They would then also be able to easily remove all of their information from a specific site once they were done using it.

Music Distribution

The music industry is likely to soon experience the biggest shakeup since the popularization of the mp3, though this one should be beneficial instead of extremely destructive. There are currently numerous different startup companies that are looking to make use of blockchain technology when it comes to how music is shared and distributed, but also the way in which artists and record labels receive royalties for the things they create.

Blockchain in this scenario can be used to ensure that the rights holders to various pieces of music are automatically paid on a per use model. What's more, smart contract technology can also be used to automate the process of searching for illegal copyright infringement.

When fully up and running the system should allow for artists to remove the middleman of distribution completely and instead be able to reach out to their fans directly and make money based on the relationships they cultivate.

Healthcare

The healthcare sector is already poised to see huge benefits when it comes to implementing blockchain technology to track individual patient records as they move throughout the hospital. Early studies have shown that this method of file transmission can lead to up to 30 percent fewer mistakes in general and a more than 50 percent reduction of mistakes during emergency situations. In addition to the transmission of files, blockchain stands to make a real difference in the ways that hospitals and the like store data and share it between disparate caregivers. Their current methods often leave holes that hackers can exploit as the infrastructure for such exchanges are often patchwork at best.

As such, healthcare facilities making the change to a distributed ledger setup would make it much easier to store relevant data and then easily share it amongst any other healthcare professional. This will, in turn, allow for more accurate and all around faster diagnosis of a wide variety of difficult to detect illnesses. There are already several different startups working in this space including

Tierion out of Connecticut and Gem out of California. The goal with this particular expression of the technology is to make it mainstream enough that everyone essentially carries their complete medical history with them wherever they go. It will also be useful regarding medical testing as test subjects can be automatically monitored and then paid for their time directly after the test has been completed.

Cloud Storage

Cloud storage is an ever-increasing market that, as of yet, has not worked out a few of its most important challenges. The biggest of these is the question of security around a company's most important data. Blockchain cloud storage can clear this hurdle as it will allow businesses to take advantage of the spare existing storage that they have lying around to generate their own cloud storage based on the existing and underutilized storage space spread out throughout the company. Studies show that the average small business has a minimum of ten terabytes of storage space that is not being utilized to the fullest and that number scales based on the number of employees a company has. It is quite feasible that most companies will be able to meet a vast majority of their total storage needs, and certainly their most sensitive storage needs without having to outsource the space at all.

What's more, as the system will be run through the company's blockchain, it would also be a simple task to utilize the personal storage space of employees and pay them for the privilege of doing so. Payments for renting this storage space would then be automatically made into the same accounts that direct deposit is already connected to.

Supply Chain Management

The supply chain management industry is likely going to experience a series of disruptions as blockchain technology becomes more and more mainstream. This is because both typically focus on recording transactions in the safest and most transparent fashion possible. Blockchain-based supply chain solutions are already popping up all over the place with Provenance, in the UK, Hijro in New York, and Skuchain in California, to name a few, all taking a whack at making traditional supply chain management obsolete.

Voting

One of the areas that are most primed for disruption in the near future is the way that voting is handled, not just the voting process itself, but everything between the point that an individual register to the moment their vote is cast. This transition is likely going to happen sooner than later as the 2016 election proved that the current system is not immune to outside influences no matter how much-elected officials wish that was or wasn't the case. Under these circumstances, it is clear why a ledger that is viewable by anyone, naturally resistant to malevolent hacking attempts and accessible from anywhere may look so appealing when it comes to making individual elections more representative of the true will of the people and thus make the world a more democratic place as a whole.

There are many different companies currently working on bringing this type of system online including Democracy Earth out of Buenos Aires, which is working on a blockchain based decentralized ledger that will serve as both an identification process and online voting system. Meanwhile, in Virginia, Follow My Vote is working on creating an online voting software that governments can get behind. In addition to making the voting process safer and easier for the public, it will also make tabulating the results a much easier and less nebulous process. The days of the absentee ballot are numbered as everyone will be able to easily add their vote to the chain over a pre-set period of time with all the votes being counted instantaneously once the voting is finished. Using smart contracts, the blockchain could even notify the winners and losers of the entire election.

Chapter 13

How Governments Throughout the World Are Responding to Blockchain

As blockchain continues to grow, there are lot of different applications that it can be used for. Some people want to see it grow more on the Bitcoin network and others would like to see more banks and other institutions start to work with this platform as well. But no matter what kind of application there is for block-chain, one thing to understand is that govern-ments all throughout the world are starting to respond in very different ways to this technol-ogy, especially regarding how it relates to Bitcoin and other cryptocurrencies.

Since blockchain is being used with Bitcoin and other digital currencies, it is available all throughout the world, and this means that many different governments are trying to fig-ure out how to respond to this technology. Some governments are embracing this kind of technology, and some have even used it as the basis of forming their own cryptocurrency. In Europe, governments are encouraging banks and other financial institutions to start using blockchain to facilitate trade and to make things easier on their customers. And then there are some governments who are trying to close down blockchain and the various online currencies because they are concerned that users are avoiding taxes or committing other criminal activities.

As we are going to discuss more in this guide, there are so many benefits that can come with using this type of technology and it is likely that those countries who choose to embrace this technology are going to be the ones that see the benefits well into the future. On the other hand, those who seem to drag their feet on it or who are trying to stop the growth will run into some tensions with the users of it, and there could be some issues down the line. So, let's take some time to look at some of the different responses to this technology throughout the world.

The United States

So, the first place we are going to get started with is in the United States and how they are responding to this technology. There are a few methods that this country has used in order to react to digital currencies, and really they are not that positive for the digital currencies or for them to grow any larger.

The first issue will come in the form of a recent sanctions bill that was approved in 2017. With this bill, the United States is mandating that some foreign governments, such as North Korea and Russia, will need to monitor the circulation of these digital currencies throughout their countries. The point that the United States says they are going for is to start measuring illicit finance trends that go through this country. The worry is that illegal transactions are going on through these digital currencies in order to fund terrorism in the United States.

This could end up adding some issues for the countries that are under the mandate. The blockchain technology has made it hard for anyone to be able to monitor the transactions that occur with digital currencies. Other than the countries trying to shut down these digital currencies, it is hard for them to catch the users since the users could easily decide to remain hidden and anonymous on the network.

Unfortunately, this is not the only type of legislation that the United States is working to pass in order to make it hard for users to stick with these digital currencies. Coinbase, which is one of the largest exchanges throughout the world for various cryptocurrencies like Bitcoin and Ethereum is currently in a fight against the IRS. According to the IRS, Coinbase is failing to comply with national tax laws because it is not collecting information on users and their profits through this exchange. Many people like to go through Coinbase because they can join the network and keep their information hidden, but the IRS is worried that these people are refusing to share that information and pay their taxes.

Big banks and the government inside of American are not that fond of the decentralized idea behind blockchain and the digital currencies that it helps run. These entities are pushing back against blockchain in the hopes that users will leave and start to go back to the banks instead. Because of this, the IRS has started to make claims against Coinbase saying that they are against national tax laws because the company makes it easier for people to evade their taxes.

So basically, the IRS is going after the anonymity that is found on the Bitcoin network and is present because of the blockchain. They want Coinbase and other exchanges inside of the United States to start providing information on the users, and if they end up being successful, it will take away one of the main benefits that come with these digital currencies and which blockchain can provide. If something does end up happening to Coinbase, it would be a disaster for Bitcoin and other digital currencies because it is the largest exchange service. People would no longer be able to exchange to use Bitcoin, and that could spell a lot of trouble.

China

The good news is that not every country is reacting like the United States to the news of blockchain and digital currencies. While it seems like the United States is intent on shutting down these digital currencies and the blockchain that goes with it, China has decided to take this in a different way. Many of those who were advocates for these digital currencies estimated that it would not take long before a national bank would join the market and decide to create its own cryptocurrency. And it is now likely that The People's Bank of China may be the first national bank to do this. There have even been some test runs of this currency to see how well it would do.

As of June 2017, the Chinese government had still been quiet about their plans, but in mid-September 2017, the drop in value for Bitcoin was estimated to be due to the beginning plans for China to get out of the Bitcoin network and start their own currency. The exact timetable has still not been released as they are working out all of the kinks, but it is estimated that many other countries are working on this kind of digital currency as well, including Palestine and Russia. It is estimated that Palestine will be next because of their location. They have had trouble creating their own money printing facilities, and this makes it hard for them to have their own printed money to circulate. But with the help of digital currencies, this would no longer be an issue.

China could choose to go with digital currencies and develop their own blockchain for a variety of reasons. First, there are quite a few citizens in China that have trouble gaining access to regular banking services. These citizens are also currently facing high fees anytime they want to make payments with other countries and using a digital currency could help to save them a lot of money in the process. And the Chinese government is all for pursuing this kind of currency because it would strengthen the Communist Party in China. And the digital currency that would be used in China would be traceable, which helps to keep corruption down to a minimum.

While it seems that the United States is trying to do everything in its power to shut down these digital currencies because they want people to use regular banks or they are worried about a bit of tax evasion, the government in China and in other countries realize that these digital currencies could actually be used to help them out, and even to help them grow their own economies.

Switzerland

Europe has taken an even different approach compared to the two that were discussed before. One of the biggest private banks in Switzerland, which goes by the name of Falcon, has already embraced the trend of Bitcoin and blockchain. This bank already allows their clients to store and trade in Bitcoin, right from their own accounts. This is a good example of how companies are starting to change the way that they look at Bitcoin and some governments have started to change up their regulations so that Bitcoin can be more widely available.

Falcon was one of the first big banks to allow their customers to use Bitcoin directly and it has helped to make this kind of technology more popular throughout all of Europe. This is not the only financial institution that has started to use this technology though. There are several banks throughout Europe, including the Bank of England, who are implementing their own blockchains. These help to speed up transactions, lower fees, and facilitate trade between different countries in a way that the traditional ledger systems are not able to do. And thanks to government regulations and willingness to go with something new that has made these so popular.

These are just a few examples of how governments are reacting throughout the world to cryptocurrency and the blockchain technology. Some are embracing it and helping their customers get more benefits, some are creating their own versions of the digital currency, and others seem to be actively working to shut it all down.

As Bitcoin and blockchain continue to grow in the future, it is likely that more reactions are going to start appearing. Many countries realize that there are a lot of benefits to using blockchain and digital currencies, and the way that they embrace these technologies in the future will make a huge difference in how both of them develop from here on out.

Chapter 14

THE FUTURE OF BLOCKCHAIN – SHAP-ING TOMORROW

There are many ways in which blockchain is able to change the future. We have already spent some time discussing how this technology is going to be developed into a lot of different platforms in the future, making it more readily available to many different industries. This alone is going to change the future of blockchain. But many other changes could occur with blockchain based on how the users would like the technology to be developed.

In Capital Markets

When it comes to capital markets, interest in blockchain has already been expanding for several years with investment in this sector doubling between 2014 and 2015 and then doing so again between 2015 and 2016. This is largely because most of the advances in this market over the past few decades have been largely in the front-office while the back and middle office have remained more or less as inefficient and cumbersome as they have been since the general best-usage computer practices were standardized sometime in the 90s. This is what leads to the confounding scenario of trading an asset instantaneously and then waiting for days for things to settle officially.

Luckily, the Linux Foundation is on the case and working to bring together capital market firms and blockchain companies to develop standards that make blockchain technology even more useful in the capital markets. Rather than completely changing the capital market infrastructure, it is more likely that blockchain technology will end up working within it in such a way that it will remove much of the current inefficiency lingering in the system. It will also allow for those in this field to offer new and improved ways of offering services to clients while regulators will find new ways to optimize settlement and execution while increasing transparency to levels that have never before been dreamed of. Much of this will be due to the way that smart contracts can work to improve efficacy at virtually every level of the process.

In Banking Sector

When it comes to looking to the future of a blockchain based banking sector, you really need to look no further than China who is the first country to create its own digital currency that can scale as needed based on the demands of the current load. While all of the details on this currency have yet to be released to the rest of the world, the information that is already available indicates that the People's Bank has already tested the currency with transactions between the People's Bank and numerous private banks. It is believed that the new currency will be rolled out along with the renminbi, though an actual timetable is unknown as of the fall of 2017.

This launch will mark a serious benchmark for cryptocurrencies and will mark the first major step towards blockchain technology going truly mainstream. The rollout of the service will also help to test the technical and logistical challenge that banks everywhere will eventually need to overcome to be successful in the post-blockchain world. It will also be interesting to see how a truly digital fiat currency will affect transaction costs as it will be the first cryptocurrency that is for all intents and purposes the same as a bank note. Finally, it also marks an extremely momentous occasion in that it marks the closest that millions of Chinese citizens have even been to having access to the type of banking services that some portion of the world takes for granted. Providing this access to those who have been denied it around the world is going to have serious worldwide repercussions whose reach is impossible to estimate.

In Digital Transactions

When it comes to digital transactions in general, it is likely that blockchain technology is going to reach a point relatively soon where its core values are tested. The United States Federal Reserve System is currently working on its own form of cryptocurrency that is tentatively being called Fedcoin. It has held several closed-door meetings with a variety of prominent members of the blockchain community, several of which have been headed by the chair of the Federal Reserve herself. Fedcoin will help to solve the problems that the US government has had with cryptocurrency for years, mainly that it is a natural outlet for those who are looking to engage in shady activities on the internet without leaving a paper trail. As such, when it premieres, Fedcoin will be promoted as an official alternative to bitcoin that users can buy into at a one to one ratio with dollars.

By and large, the Fedcoin blockchain will work in just the same way that the standard cryptocurrency blockchain works now, but with a few important differences. First, each Fedcoin account will be tied to information that the government has access to, making anonymity a thing of the past and destroying one of the primary things that made people want to use it in the first place. This will also have the effect of putting a timer on the end of paper money which is also difficult to track in most instances. Additionally, the Federal Reserve will have full control over the Fedcoin blockchain which means that if they do not like a particular transaction they can simply delete it from the blockchain and revert the funds back to their original location. The public reception to the rollout of this currency will determine a lot about the way that blockchain technology will be used for digital transactions in the future.

In Real Estate

Real estate transactions are some of the most notoriously painstaking and tedious that you can try to undertake, mainly due to the lack of innovation in the industry over the past few decades. Luckily, blockchain technology will soon be poised to rectify this lack of technology advancement. Blockchain technology stands poised to revolutionize the entire listing process, cutting listing services and property agents largely out of the loop. Instead, blockchain will make possible a type of decentralized platform when firms, agents, sellers, and buyers can both list and complete real estate transactions around the world with few, if any, of the traditional hassles getting in the way of the process.

By getting rid of the traditional centralized structure, the system will provide those in the real estate industry a greater access to a wide variety of fee structures that they will have far more control over. What's more, as the entire database will be decentralized, the listings will be free for everyone to use without any of the standard restrictions or paywalls. This will ensure that buyers have access to better data and that sellers have access to the greatest number of interested buyers possible.

In Public Benefits

The public service sector is an extremely complex system in that it is centralized when it comes to its responsibility in carrying out the delivery of public services while also remaining fragmented in the way that each service is actually carried out and how various departments share data. The effects of this duality typically cut deep as departmental budgets are slashed, and questions arise over decreasing services or changing the way in which they are delivered.

As blockchain technology becomes more mainstream, it is likely that it will be used more and more frequently when it comes to addressing the inefficacy of the current system head-on. When given the change, blockchain technology will easily serve as the official registry for a wide variety of assets that require a government license, along with any intellectual property the agency might own. It will also prove useful when it comes to streamlining and coordinating purchasing, making each governmental dollar stretch as far as it possibly can and resulting in a surplus that can be used on the public in the process.

In all of these situations, blockchain technology will certainly improve response times and reduce the risk of errors or fraud which also enhance productivity and efficiency at all levels of the process. Essentially, anywhere there is government inefficiency, blockchain technology can help to stamp it out.

In Industries

Modern business runs more or less smoothly based on the work of a wide variety of administrators who manage the databases and record the numbers. Supervisory boards, auditors, solicitors, auditing firms and even much of the financial sector all exist based on the need for third-party verification of a transaction between two accounts. As such, the biggest potential disruption that blockchain may cause is to remove the need for third-party verification services outside of its own. This has the potential to be a momentous change for any industry that requires verification of payments, which is to say all of them.

This verification process is going to sow change across a vast number of industries; distributed ledgers offer a chance to improve the level of trust and truth in every single system to which it applies. The very idea that you can prove in a moment exactly who owns, what is going to affect everything that currently exists as a means of verifying performance, payments ownership and contracts will all soon find itself switched to blockchain.

This will result in a severe shift in power from those who are currently in charge of managing these transactions, though it will likely not benefit new businesses as much as one might expect. Instead, it will be existing businesses, which can leverage the trust that they already have, combined with the new and improved means of doing business, to ensure that they end up in a new and more profitable position than they were currently in.

Conclusion

Thank you for making it through to the end of this book, let's hope it was informative and able to provide you with all of the tools you need to achieve your goals, whatever it is that they may be. Just because you have finished this book does not mean there is nothing left to learn on the topic, expanding your horizons is the only way to find the mastery you seek. As blockchain is still such a new technology, there is no telling when new potentially game-changing information is going to emerge which means keeping your ear to the ground is the only way to actually ensure that you are not caught off guard.

The next step is to stop reading already and to start considering all the ways that blockchain technology can potentially change your life. When it comes to putting it to use for your business, then it is important to keep in mind that only a handful of business is going to ride into prominence on blockchain's back which means it is far better to instead consider the way that you can put the technology to work in order to enhance the already effective aspects of your business even more.

If you are an individual who is still considering the best way to start taking advantage of blockchain for business purposes, then the next thing you are going to do is to get in-volved with the blockchain community as much as possible. The more you interact with the community and do your part to promote blockchain technology across all walks of life, the more you will create opportunities for yourself in the future when it comes to finding a paying niche in the overall blockchain tapestry. The more people you meet when working for free, the more doors you will find open to you later on.

Finally, before you go, I'd like to say "thank you" for purchasing my book.

I know you could have picked from dozens of books on this topic, but you took a chance with my guide. So, big thanks for downloading this book and reading all the way to the end.

Additional Resources

www.techrepublic.com/videos/what-blockchain-means-to-the-enterprise/

www.techrepublic.com/article/blockchain-the-smart-persons-guide/

www.techrepublic.com/article/why-your-next-storage-solution-may-depend-on-blockchain/

www.techproresearch.com/article/why-the-blockchain-belongs-on-the-cxo-roadmap/

www.techproresearch.com/downloads/it-leader-s-guide-to-the-blockchain/

www.cnet.com/news/ibm-blockchain-bitcoins-technology-surprising-fan/

www.techrepublic.com/article/ibm-watson-fda-to-use-blockchain-tech-to-build-secure-exchange-for-health-data/

www.techrepublic.com/resource-library/webcasts/revolutionizing-it-with-block-chain-and-cloud-computing/

www.zdnet.com/article/second-thoughts-on-blockchain/

www.zdnet.com/article/blockchain-unblocked-its-implications-for-enterprise-computing/

www.techrepublic.com/article/why-your-next-storage-solution-may-depend-on-blockchain/

www.techrepublic.com/article/video-the-top-5-things-to-know-about-the-blockchain/

BITCOIN

Mastering Bitcoin for Beginners

How You Can Make Insane Money Investing and Trading in Bitcoin

Introduction

Congratulations on downloading this book and thank you for doing so.

OK, so what's Bitcoin?

It's not an actual coin, it's "cryptocurrency," a digital form of payment that is produced ("mined") by lots of people worldwide. It allows peer-to-peer transactions instantly, worldwide, for free or at very low cost.

Bitcoin is now deemed to be the foremost payment procedure for online commerce, ardent spectators of cryptocurrencies consider this fact to be a drastic march on the trails of finance viewed on a universal scale. Experts however, spark a fresh debate around and on the matter of Bitcoin, simply the fact that majority of buyers in Bitcoin market are a bunch of speculators. Bitcoin is an ideal reflection of how cryptocurrencies can assume a shape in the imminent time, and capitalists must deem a larger perspective. The immense popularity and ever-mounting price is momentary, but dealing with the essentials regarding Bitcoin and its trivial competitors will lead to a perfect deliberation and that's going to determine its imminent future.

The following chapters will take it slow and start out by discussing the basics of bitcoin and describing how it works in simple terms so that everything is on the same page when it comes to the details. This information will then be built upon with a discussion of how bitcoin can be used successfully along with its pros and cons. Next, you will learn all about how bitcoin and blockchain technology is on track to reshape financial services and why cryptocurrency is so important to a wide swath of the globe.

From there you will learn about several different apps that are well on their way to shaping the future before taking a more in-depth look at the specifics behind bitcoin and blockchain. Then you will learn about how you can buy/sell and invest in bitcoin and how to make insane money trading bitcoin. Finally, you will learn about how I became a crypto millionaire in 6 months trading cryptocurrency and bitcoin.

There are plenty of books on this subject on the market, thanks again for choosing this one! Every effort was made to ensure it is full of as much useful information as possible, please enjoy!

Chapter 1

Introducing Bitcoin

What Is Bitcoin?

We live in a world where almost everything is centralized. To obtain food, most people don't go to a farm that is owned and run by a family. Instead, they usually go to a grocery store and buy food that was grown on large, corporately-owned fields in another country. The coffee that you buy was probably produced from beans grown in South America or Indonesia on a plantation owned by a large corporation. That corporation probably paid workers little amounts of money for them to work the fields. The end product of ground coffee was perhaps shipped to a centralized warehouse — say, a Folgers or Maxwell House warehouse — then distributed it to stores that are corporately owned by a central organization. If you bought the coffee at Wal-Mart, you bought it from a centralized organization that does not do commerce on a local level.

Unless you take care to make sure that the cloth used to make your clothes were obtained from a local place and then sewn by a local seamstress or tailor, your clothes were probably produced in the same way. The fibers used to create the cloth were probably grown on a large plantation in a poor part of the world, and workers were paid slave wages to tend to it. Another set of workers toiled in sweatshops, making pennies for their time and energy, to turn the fiber into fabric and then the fabric into clothes. By the time the clothes made their way to you, the consumer, and the centralized company that produces the clothes — say, Gap, Old Navy, JCPenney, or Nike — has made a tremendous profit.

Banks and other financial institutions run in a similar fashion. Money is generated by the United States government, either in the form of cash or interest rates. If the government wishes to increase the amount of money in circulation, it can either print more cash or lower interest rates. If it wishes to decrease the amount of money in circulation, it can either destroy cash or raise interest rates. Moreover, the central government can determine precisely how much the dollars that it creates are worth. It can devalue the dollar so that it loses power against other currency, or implement policies to increase the dollar's value against other currencies. Every move that it makes regarding fiscal policy directly impacts every person who uses dollars; the individuals who use the dollars have little say in what the centralized government is doing about the value of their dollars.

Most individuals and companies choose to keep their dollars in banks for safekeeping and growth. Those banks are again centralized locations. Some banks, like Chase and Wells Fargo, are huge conglomerations that have local branches to service customers in particular geographical areas. Other banks like local credit unions have policies designed to benefit the local economy but still are out to maintain their own bottom line. In other words, money goes to the banks so that ultimately the banks, not the individual customers can benefit.

Bitcoin presents an entirely new paradigm, a shift away from the culture of centralization so that power goes back to the individual people involved in the economy rather than to entities at the center who stand to get rich. It is a form of money that is not run by a government or a bank but instead run by the individual people who use it. In other words, it is decentralized. While there is a team of developers who are adding to the Bitcoin code and protocol, they are unable to manipulate it in any way. They don't control it and nobody controls it. It is a revolution against the control brought about by centralization.

Bitcoin is a type of virtual currency, also referred to as a cryptocurrency. Virtual currencies are types of money that exist entirely in a digital form rather than as cash that can be carried around. It was originally conceived of as a peer-to-peer currency system, making it vastly different than fiat currencies that are regulated by a centralized government (for more information on the differences between

Bitcoin and normal currencies, see Chapter 3). It is unregulated, meaning that because national governments do not issue it, they are not able to pass laws controlling it. More than just a currency, it is a movement that has empowered people to take control of their own economics and finances without having to pay taxes or governments telling them what their money is worth and what they can and can't do with it.

Bitcoin runs on a type of technology called blockchain; blockchain was actually invented as the means by which Bitcoin would run. It ushered in a new era of computer programming in which systems can be virtually 100% hack-proof (for more information on the blockchain, see Chapter 2).

History of Bitcoin

Bitcoin was originally conceived by an anonymous individual (or group of individuals) who went by the pseudonym, Satoshi Nakamoto. On October 31, 2008, Nakamoto (who will from this point forward be referred to as a "he," simply for ease of reference) released a white paper detailing the concept behind a cryptocurrency that would be upheld through a new technology known as blockchain. However, there were some important developments in the history of cybersecurity and programming that served as important precedents to his conception.

During the 1980s and especially in the 1990s, computer technology was advancing at a rapid rate, especially in the area of graphics editing. Images of models in advertisements could be airbrushed to make them appear slimmer, taller, and younger than they actually were; this phenomenon led to the legal and ethical concern of digital information being manipulated. If there was no way to prove beyond reasonable doubt that information stored on a computer had not been tampered with, then that information could not be used as evidence in a court of law. Furthermore, companies could easily manipulate the information held on their computers, which no one would be aware of. They could foreseeably backdate contracts so that certain terms could not be applied, change the dates of transactions that had occurred, and even manipulate accounting data to make the company appear to be worth more than it actually was. In early 1991, two computer programmers, W. Scott Stornetta and Stuart Haber, published an article entitled "How to Time-Stamp a Digital Document" in the *Journal of Cryptology*. In the article, they described a method that they had come up within which the data itself, rather than the document containing the data, would be time-stamped in a way that could not be tampered with, even by a professional third-party time-stamp service. Their idea helped form the time-stamp feature of the blockchain technology used to create Bitcoin, which helps to ensure that transactions made using the currency cannot be manipulated.

When the Internet came to prominence in the 1990s and began to revolutionize the way that business was done, security breaches that cost companies thousands, if not millions of dollars began to become almost commonplace. Hackers found ways to break into the central servers that housed all of a company's information and were able to siphon off not only large sums of money but also personal information — bank account and credit card numbers, addresses, birthdates, social security numbers — of private customers. A computer security expert at the University of Cambridge named Ross Anderson published multiple papers throughout the 1990s and into the 2000s regarding problems related to cybersecurity. He made the case that the need wasn't for tighter security protocols but for a complete change in how cybersecurity was done. The current network model in which people accessed a website by connecting to the main server which was severely inadequate. If the main server, which housed all of the company's information was hacked, the entire system would fail. The need was to move away from this network model to one that was much less susceptible to hacking.

During the time that Anderson was pushing for a paradigm shift in cybersecurity protocols, a programmer named Michael Doyle created a mechanism for ensuring chain-of-evidence protocols on digital systems. Chain of evidence is important in any legal situation because a court needs to verify whether or not that evidence has been tampered with. Individuals who have handled evidence need to carefully document when they had that evidence and what they did with it. However, as with the problem of data manipulation that Haber and Stornetta proposed a solution for, there was no foolproof way to ensure that chain-of-evidence protocol had been followed with digital information. In 1998, Doyle filed for a patent for a program that would ensure that chain-of-evidence protocol was followed with digital information. His invention used a set of public and private keys, another feature that would be essential in the development of blockchain technology and Bitcoin.

Also in 1998, a computer programmer named Nick Szabo proposed a protocol for a digital currency program that he referred to as bit gold. Bit gold would theoretically exist in an entirely cashless state. Rather than its value being assigned artificially by the government, it would be determined by the laws of supply and demand; the number of bit gold users would determine how high the demand was, thereby giving it its value. It would employ chain-of-evidence protocols and time-stamp to ensure that the digital information through which the currency existed could not be manipulated. Bit gold users would work together to solve complex puzzles; the solutions would unlock more bit gold and become part of the next puzzle. This procedure would allow bit gold to create a peer-to-peer chain in which none of the information could be retroactively altered without every single person on the bit gold network colluding to change it. Bit gold was never implemented, but its design was so closely linked to that of Bitcoin that many have suggested Szabo could actually be the figure behind the pseudonym, Satoshi Nakamoto.

Fast-forward 10 years, to August of 2008. Three programmers named Neal King, Vladimir Oksman, and Charles Bry filed for a patent for a new encryption technology that built on the public and private keys that Michael Doyle created. The patent is almost an exact copy of the blockchain technology that Nakamoto would introduce two months later. However, the three men deny any connection to Nakamoto.

The Bitcoin white paper was the product of nearly two decades of advances in the field of cybersecurity, and it built on many pre-existing ideas. The centralized server system is prone to hacking, no matter how intense security protocols may be; banks that use a centralized server set all of their customers at risk of losing money and personal information. Bitcoin is different, it was created by developing an entirely new model of programming and cybersecurity, one which is insusceptible to hacking and data manipulation. Nakamoto

set out to create a peer-to-peer virtual currency that would change how money is handled,
and in the process also created a programming
model that would change the paradigm of system security.

Just as the blockchain technology that under-
lies Bitcoin, it was not created in isolation, the
Bitcoin revolution did not happen overnight
but took several years and failures. On January
3, 2009, Bitcoin was officially launched when
Nakamoto mined the "genesis block" (for more
information on mining, see Chapter 4; for
more information on what a block is, see
Chapter 2). It was not a public moment that
led to standing ovations; at least, not at first.
In fact, for several years, Bitcoin was little
more than a side interest of the technophile
community. However, members of that community developed an interest in the concept of
blockchain and Bitcoin and helped lay the
foundation for its development as an economic
revolution.

On October 5, 2009 — over a year and a half
after it was initially released — a user known
as New Liberty Standard published an exchange rate for Bitcoin: 1.309.03 BTC per dollar, or about .08 cents each. This rate was not
based on how much in demand the virtual currency was because up until this point, it had
never even been used as a monetary currency.
Rather, it was based on how much electricity
was required to mine one Bitcoin.

The year 2010 saw Bitcoin begin to show its viability in the commercial sector. In May of that year, Laszlo Hanyecz offered 10,000 Bitcoins to anyone who would order him two large pizzas. A user known as jercos took him up on that offer and ordered the pizzas from Papa Johns. This event marked the first time that Bitcoin was used in a commercial transaction. That summer, Bitcoin 0.3 was published on the technophile news website www.slashdot.com, which caused a surge of popularity. A man named Jed McCaleb grabbed onto the concept and established a Bitcoin wallet, which would come to be known as Mt. Gox. Mt. Gox would become a financial giant before collapsing in a scandal that would threaten to sink the entire concept of crypto-currency. By the end of 2010, the total value of all Bitcoins in circulation would exceed one million dollars.

However, not all was good news. That same year, an international watchdog known as the Financial Action Task Force issued a warning for virtual currencies. The anonymity associated with them, as opposed to the verification processes required by many banks could be exploited to support illicit activities such as money laundering and terrorism. Sadly, that prediction would soon prove to be true. On January 27, 2011, Ross Ulbricht created a web-site known as Silk Road, an illicit website named after the ancient trade route that connected China to the West. His goal was to use

Bitcoin's anonymity to enable people to purchase illegal drugs online.

In the third quarter of 2010, a Bitcoin user suggested that because of its anonymity, Bitcoin is used to fund the controversial WikiLeaks page. PayPal, MasterCard, Discover, Visa, and other major payment processors had made contributions to WikiLeaks using their accounts impossible, so Bitcoin seemed to be the perfection option. However, on December 5, Satoshi Nakamoto stated that he did not wish to take a political stance because assessing controversial situations such as WikiLeaks was not the best way to grow the currency. A week later, he made his final appearance in the Bitcoin community before the pseudonym disappeared altogether. Despite his admonitions, Bitcoin enthusiasts used the currency to contribute tens of thousands of dollars to WikiLeaks.

With Nakamoto no longer a part of the Bitcoin community (other than his massive Bitcoin holdings), it lacked a visionary leader to guide it. While Bitcoin was created to be decentralized rather than function around any galvanizing force, Nakamoto's vision had been an essential part of moving forward the virtual currency movement. The year 2011 would see the ramifications of his absence, as Bitcoin scandals began to erupt. Most notably was the Silk Road website, but Bitcoin was also used by so-called entrepreneurs to engage in money laundering.

Bitcoin grew considerably during 2011. In February, it reached parity with the US dollar, meaning that one Bitcoin was worth one dollar. The next month, Britcoin was established to facilitate trade between Bitcoins and British pounds, and an exchange opened in Brazil to facilitate trade between Bitcoins and Brazilian reals. By April, Bitcoins could be exchanged with Eurodollars and had parity with the pound sterling and Euro.

On April 16, 2011, edition of *Time Magazine* featured an article by journalist Jerry Brito entitled "Online Cash Bitcoin Could Challenge Government, Banks." It was the first time that Bitcoin was featured in a mainstream news outlet and led to such a high surge in its popularity that by the summer, one Bitcoin was worth ten dollars.

That same summer, Mt. Gox was hacked; the hacker transferred to himself a large number of Bitcoins that did not exist, and the value of one Bitcoin was falsely lowered to one cent. Mt. Gox and other exchanges quickly responded with tighter security measures. This event revealed that while Bitcoin itself was impregnable, the exchanges that facilitated its use were not. Another event would soon unfold that would show that even though the US government does not regulate Bitcoin, it will prosecute people who use it to engage in money laundering.

In August of 2011, so-called entrepreneurs Charlie Shrem and Gareth Nelson created a startup called BitInstant. BitInstant claimed that it was able to enact high-speed transactions, which would otherwise take an hour or more to process. In 2014, the company was found to be engaging in money laundering, and the FBI got involved in the prosecution. In November of 2011, Trendon Shavers opened the Bitcoin Savings and Trust, which promised high-yield investments of 7%, meaning that in addition to the rapidly increasing value of Bitcoin's exchange value, the number of Bitcoins that an investor-owned would double every ten weeks. This company was revealed to be a Ponzi scheme, and investors were defrauded out of 700,000, with total damages estimated at $40 million. Events such as these threatened to derail the entire Bitcoin movement.

Nevertheless, it continued to gain steam with the public and the commercial sector. In November of 2013, a research article came out which showed that while in the early years of Bitcoin, the currency was used for illicit "sin activities," it is now a legitimate currency that is mainly used for commercial purchases of everyday goods. More and more retailers began accepting payments in Bitcoins, and in November 2013, the University of Nicosia in Cyprus started accepting Bitcoins as payment for tuition. They could even be used for large purchases, such as a house or car.

Another tragedy erupted in early 2014 that once again, threatened to derail Bitcoin completely. Mt. Gox, now the largest Bitcoin exchange in the world began bankruptcy proceedings. It was now insolvent because a theft that occurred in 2011 had led to the loss of over 700, 00 Bitcoins. Many investors lost thousands of dollars' worth of Bitcoins, and total losses were estimated to be half a billion dollars.

Over the next few years, as the Bitcoin movement continued to grow with increasing force, governments began making moves to try to regulate the cryptocurrency. New York State required companies to get an expensive BitLicense before they could accept payments in Bitcoins, and the IRS issued a statement that Bitcoins were considered assets, a move that could lead to taxes on them. The government of Japan allowed for payments in Bitcoins to the government, and the currency began to be accepted by UK banks such as Barclays. While the latter moves look like openings for Bitcoins to be accepted more in the mainstream, some are concerned that they are underhanded attempts at regulation.

Despite numerous setbacks, the Bitcoin community has continued to grow, continually defying the predictions set by mainstream economists and politicians. As a movement, it shows no signs of stopping.

How to Get Your First Bitcoins

Whatever your reasons for wanting to become involved in the Bitcoin movement, the decision is one that you are not likely to regret.

Its growth cannot be matched by any mainstream investments, and while you may not become a millionaire overnight (but hey, you could), if you are willing to ride out the ups and downs of virtual currency, you stand a very good chance of watching your money grow.

There are several different ways to get your first Bitcoin. Before you can do so, you will need a Bitcoin wallet (for more information on Bitcoin wallets, see Chapter 5), which makes you a part of the Bitcoin blockchain so that you can send and receive Bitcoins.

One way to get your first Bitcoins is to request to be paid in Bitcoins. If a friend or family member wants to send you money for your birthday, graduation, or other special occasions, ask that they sent it to you in Bitcoins rather than in dollars or another national currency. If you own an online business, you can enable customers to pay with Bitcoins. BitPay is a tool that will allow you to do this. To get started with BitPay, go to www.bitpay.com.

You will need to have a Bitcoin wallet already so that you can connect it to the BitPay tool. The website will guide you through the simple process of enabling Bitcoin-based payments on your website.

Another way to get your first Bitcoin is to buy them through an exchange. There are many Bitcoin exchanges, and they each come with their own benefits and drawbacks. Local-BitCoins is an exchange that allows users in the same geographical area to arrange a time and place to meet so that they can exchange Bitcoins in person. Kraken and CoinMama are just a couple of online exchanges through which you can buy Bitcoins with dollars or other national currencies. While secure, exchanges can have very high fees, so make sure that you are aware of the fees before you make your purchase.

Sending and Receiving Bitcoin

Sending and receiving Bitcoins is a relatively simple, easy process. There are two ways in which you can send Bitcoins. One is if you already have the Bitcoins in your wallet, and the second is if you don't. Either way, you will need to know the public key for the person to whom you are sending the Bitcoins (for more information on public keys, see Chapter 2). If you already have the Bitcoins in your wallet, you will simply go to your wallet and select the option in the menu that allows you to send

Bitcoins. You will then be prompted to enter the amount that you want to send and the public key specifying where they will be sent. Once you complete the transaction, the blockchain will take from about 10 minutes to one hour to verify it. Once it is verified, the other person will receive an email with the Bitcoins. If you do not already have the Bitcoins in your wallet, you will need to purchase them as part of the sending process. Go to your wallet and select the option in the menu that allows you to send Bitcoins.

You will need to enter the amount and the public key, as well as the payment information that you will be using to pay for the Bitcoins.

The blockchain will need to verify both your purchase of the Bitcoins and the sending of them to the other person, so the transaction may take up to two hours to process. Once it is fully processed, the other person will receive an email saying that you sent him or her Bitcoins.

Chapter 2

How the Bitcoin Protocol Works?

Bitcoin runs on a technology called blockchain; blockchain was actually created to facilitate the cryptocurrency. Before getting into details about how the Bitcoin protocol works, this chapter will explain some about blockchain.

A ledger is a record of transactions that have occurred within an account. For example, your bank and credit card statements are both ledgers. Accountants use ledgers to keep track of a company's finances. The blockchain is, at its core, a digital ledger. This means that it is basically a collection of transactions that are linked together in a continuous chain. Groups of transactions are collected into sections known as "blocks." Those blocks are connected into a chain, hence the term "blockchain."

Blockchain Transactions

Traditionally, computer programs are run through the server model. This means that whenever you get onto a website, you are actually connecting to that website's main server, which stores all of its information. If there is a problem with the server, the website will not work. When a website is down for maintenance, the reason is usually because work needs to be done on that server. If anyone hacks into that server, all of the information on that website could be compromised. This is a huge problem when that website contains sensitive information; imagine someone hacking into your bank's main server and stealing all of the information associated with your account.

Blockchain runs differently. Instead of the program being connected to one central server, it runs on a series of nodes. Nodes are individual computers, usually operated by private individuals that are a part of the network and contain all of the information on the blockchain. This means that instead of hacking into one computer, a hacker would have to be able to access every single node simultaneously. The only other way for a security breach to occur is for every single node operator to be in collusion. Considering that many blockchains, including Bitcoin, run on thousands of nodes, the odds of that scenario happening are extremely low. Therefore, blockchain is virtually impenetrable to hackers.

Because so many nodes are involved in executing the program, blockchain runs as open-source software. This means that the codes are publicly available and anyone has access to them. Furthermore, all of the transactions that occur on the digital ledger are made public for everyone to see; however, the identities of those involved in the transactions are anonymous. The open-source, public nature of blockchain means that no one can manipulate any of the information. While companies such as Enron failed because of secretive and illegal accounting practices that were not discovered until it was too late, blockchain makes that possibility impossible.

That explains some of the basic concepts behind blockchain. It is a decentralized, open-source software that is inaccessible to hackers or manipulators. This next section will explain some more technical details on how it actually works.

As previously mentioned, groups of transactions are collected together into blocks. Each block is time-stamped, similarly to the method proposed by Haber and Stornetta in 1991, to show that the information in that block was present at the time of its verification. The timestamp is used to generate something called a hash value, which is publicly broadcasted. A hash is basically a summary of large amounts of information in the blockchain, the hash is an alphanumeric value that converts the input message (the information in the block) into a cryptographic puzzle. This is also known as the digital fingerprint because, like fingerprints, no two hash values are the same. Miners, people who solve the cryptographic puzzles in exchange for rewards, compete against each other to solve the puzzle created by the hash. The solution becomes a part of the hash in the next block, thereby linking all the blocks into one continuous algorithm.

When a user wishes to make a transaction on a blockchain, say, Jack wants to send Jill two Bitcoins, he must do so using Jill's public key and his own private key. This creates an input value and generates a digital signature. Once the digital signature is used to authorize the transaction, the data becomes embedded in a block. The input value is converted into an output value. This output is used to derive the user's public key from the private key; the public key then uses an algorithm to transform itself via a hash function into a unique value, thereby creating the sending user's public address that is visible on the blockchain's nodes.

The block is then sent to the nodes for verification via solving the cryptographic function created by the hash. This process of verification ensures that the transactions in that block did take place. Once verified, the block becomes a part of the blockchain. Consequent, blocks that are verified are linked to it, making going back to change the information in the block that contains Jack and Jill's transaction impossible. Jill then receives an email saying that Jack has sent her two Bitcoins, and the ownership of those two Bitcoins is conferred to her. The entire transaction process can take up to an hour or more, but the tradeoff is the high level of security inherent in the blockchain protocols.

Bitcoin Transactions

Here is a diagram of how the Bitcoin protocol works, laid out in Satoshi Nakamoto's white paper.

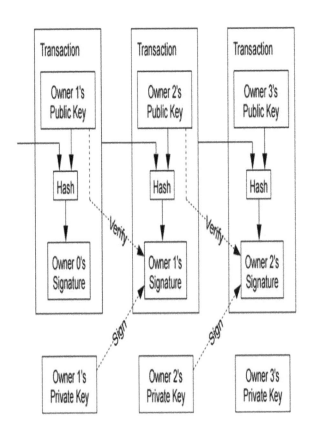

As the diagram shows, when someone wants to initiate a Bitcoin transaction, that person's public key is applied to the solution from the previous block to generate a new hash that

must be solved for that transaction to be verified. The digital signature, aka private key
from the previous transaction — generated
from the hash of the previous block — is applied as part of the verification process. When
the next person wants to make a transaction,
that person's public key is combined with the
solution from the previous block to create a
new hash.

The previous person's private key is applied to
create the new digital process, which again is
used for the next transaction. Because all of
the transactions are connected, none of the
information can be changed without retroactively changing every other transaction that
precedes it in the blockchain.

Bitcoin Mining Transactions

Mining is the process whereby virtual currency, such as Bitcoins, are generated and added
to the existing pool. Nodes on the blockchain
network are used to create the cryptographic
hash puzzle that must be solved for a transaction to be verified; miners compete with each
other to solve the puzzle. Whoever solves it
first gets a reward, usually a predetermined
amount of the virtual currency. Once solved,
the hash is re-converted into the input message, which is publicly visible as part of the
blockchain. This process allows the blocks to
be verified. For more information on Bitcoin
mining, see Chapter 5.

Chapter 3

HOW BITCOIN IS DIFFERENT FROM NATIONAL CURRENCIES

This chapter will look at what currency is and what money is as a means of dispelling some of the myths about money. The goal is to show how Bitcoin, while substantially different from national currencies, is actually a purer form of money than what is minted by many governments.

Currency

Currency is simply a medium of exchange. Imagine that Jim's mother packed him a hamburger for lunch, and John's mother packed him a hotdog for lunch. In the school cafeteria, John looks at Jim's hamburger and decides that he would rather have that than his hotdog. He tells Jim that he will trade him his hotdog for Jim's hamburger. Fortunately for John, Jim has been eyeing the hotdog enviously and wanted to eat it for his lunch. Jim agrees to the offer, and the two make the exchange. In this scenario, food was the medium of exchange or the currency that was used to make sure that each of the boys got the lunch that they desired.

This process of exchanging via an agreed-upon currency has been viewed by some anthropologists as what sets humans apart from other animals. The beginning of currency was essentially the beginning of human civilization; in other words, when a group of people began trading, they began to develop a civilization. Say that an ancient merchant traveling from modern-day Iran to modern-day Turkey has many goods, including silks, rugs, and spices, loaded on his camels. He arrives in Turkey and finds a shopkeeper who specializes in selling oriental rugs. He has a collection of emerald jewels and pearls that he offers in exchange for the rugs that the Persian merchant is selling. The merchant agrees to the exchange, and when the shopkeeper pays for the rugs, their ownership is transferred to him. In this scenario, the emeralds and pearls were the currency that both men agreed to use for the exchange. What would have happened if the merchant did not agree to that particular currency? Either the shopkeeper would have had to find a different currency; say, exquisite beads, gold, or silver, or the exchange would not have been able to occur.

In saying that Bitcoin is a currency, this simply means that it is a medium of exchange that individuals or other entities (such as businesses) can choose to accept or not accept in exchange for goods and services.

Money as Currency

Money is a unique type of currency that has a fixed value. As trade began to expand across civilizations, there was a need for traders to be able to exchange with a currency that was more universal so would be accepted in many different places. That currency usually came in the form of gold, silver, and other valuable metals. The Turkish shopkeeper could keep on hand a certain amount of gold and use it to exchange for any goods that merchants may be bringing, whether those merchants came from Ethiopia, Iran, China, or the Levant. Instead of looking for something of value to offer in exchange for oriental rugs, a fixed amount of gold would be the price for whatever the merchants were selling.

As societies grew and governments developed into more stable and more powerful institutions, they began using precious metals and other valuable metals, such as bronze and nickel to mint coins that would be worth a certain amount.

Those coins could be used not only for people to pay each other for goods and services but also for them to pay taxes to the government. In other words, national mints developed as a means for governments to exploit the people for taxes. Merchants traveling between different societies could still carry gold coins of a universal value, or they could carry local coins and try to exchange them when they reached different places.

Fast-forward to the end of the Middle Ages, when European explorers were traveling to lands as far away as China. Marco Polo noticed that instead of carrying purses full of heavy coins, Chinese people carried notes of paper which were redeemable for a certain amount. These notes were similar to what we today refer to as "cash." They had no intrinsic value of their own, other than the paper on which they were printed. However, the government and bank that issued them guaranteed that they were worth a certain amount. Marco Polo returned to Europe and told people about the monetary system that the Chinese used, and people laughed at him because the system seemed to be so unreasonable. After all, how could the government guarantee that a piece of paper had a certain value? People were much more comfortable sticking with coins.

In the second half of the 17th century, the Bank of Sweden decided to experiment with issuing paper notes instead of coins. Anyone who was in possession of a banknote could redeem it to the bank for a certain amount of gold or silver. However, if the bank were to fail, the banknotes would become worthless. England soon followed suit when the Bank of England began issuing banknotes as a form of debt against the Crown. In other words, the king or queen owed money to whoever was in possession of banknotes. Put simply, the modern monetary system that we use is basically an elaborate form of debt between the government and private individuals.

The system of using banknotes that were guaranteed by the central bank or treasury and regulated by the central government spread throughout Europe and the New World. For several hundred years, they were backed by what was known as either the gold or silver standard. This meant that the central bank had to keep in reserve enough gold or silver to uphold the value of the money so that if every single citizen were to redeem all of their banknotes, they would be able to receive a proportional amount of gold or silver. Under the Nixon administration, the gold standard was dropped. This means that the central bank is no longer able to redeem the value printed on the banknotes for a certain amount. Their value is not determined by how much gold one can get for them but by what the government says that they are worth. This new concept is referred to as "fiat currency." Fiat means faith, and to use the money issued by a government, you have to have faith that the government will uphold its value.

Today, every national government has its own form of money that it mints. Brazil has the real, India has the rupee, the United States has the dollar, the United Kingdom has the pound sterling, the European Union has the Euro,

Turkey has the Lyra, Jordan has the Dinar. Moreover, governments can manipulate the money that they issue in more ways than ever before. They can control how much is in circulation by either printing or destroying cash. They can determine its value by raising or lowering interest rates, thereby artificially inflating or deflating how much someone can buy with his or her money.

Bitcoin as Currency

The fact that Bitcoins are not minted by a central government does not mean that they are worthless. Going back to a basic understanding, it shows that the fact that they aren't minted by a central government means that they are actually a more legitimate form of currency than dollars, Euros, or other national forms of money.

Keep in mind that currency is simply a medium of exchange that two parties in a transaction can agree upon. While dollars are by far the most ubiquitous currency used in the United States (you can go to any store and buy anything there with dollars), but they are not the only means of negotiating payment. For example; if a person orders food at a restaurant and after enjoying a lovely dinner for which he has no money, he will probably be forced to go to the kitchen and wash dishes until he has covered the cost of his meal. While this situation is probably humiliating for both the diner and restaurant manager, it shows that even without the presence of dollars, the food can be paid for, in this situation with work.

So, what if there was another form of currency, other than dollars, that carries a certain value across different settings that people in the United States could still use to pay for things? That currency exists and it is called Bitcoin.

he fact that Bitcoins are not minted by any central government caring with it heavy implications for how Bitcoin works, as opposed to how national currencies work. The value of national currencies is regulated by the government that mints them. The value of Bitcoin is determined by the people who use it. Central to any economic theory lies the laws of supply and demand. Supply refers to how much of something is available, and demand refers to how much of it people want. If the store has a supply of 10 apples, but I need (demand) 12 apples, then the supply is lower than the demand. Imagine that I am going to that store with my brother, who also needs 12 apples. Now, not only the supply much smaller than the demand, but I will have to fight with my brother for the apples. Imagine now that the shopkeeper is rather shrewd, and seeing the impending meltdown, takes away all of the apples and raises the price. They are now three times what they originally cost. He also tells my brother and me that we had better act like civilized people in his shop. Neither one of us wants to pay that much money for 12 measly apples (which were probably genetically modified), so we each begrudgingly take 5 and pay for them. To make up for the deficit, I get 7 oranges, and my brother gets 7 pears. Why was the shopkeeper able to raise the price of the apples so high and we're still willing to pay for them? Because of what they were worth to us. They were not intrinsically connected to a certain dollar figure; they do not have a universal value. Rather, because we really wanted them and there weren't enough available, we were willing to pay more for them.

The value of Bitcoin is determined by what it is worth to the people who use it. If a lot of people want to buy Bitcoins, their value will increase. If Bitcoins get dumped so that there is a surplus in circulation, their value will drop. While governments artificially determine the value of national currencies, the value of Bitcoin is determined exclusively through the economic mainstay of supply and demand. Even without a regulating body, as long as people want Bitcoin, it will have value.

In addition to not being able to be regulated, as of right now, Bitcoin is not able to be taxed, at least not in the same way as the national currency. The IRS has declared that Bitcoin is an asset, like property, and should be taxed as such based on gains and losses. However, it is not taxed the same way that your paycheck is taxed.

In short, Bitcoin is better than national currencies because it takes power away from the centralized government and puts it back into the hands of the common people. The value of Bitcoin cannot be manipulated by any central institution but rather is determined as it should be: through the laws of supply and demand.

Chapter 4

UNDERSTANDING THE BLOCKCHAIN TECHNOLOGY

At its most basic, a blockchain is a type of de-centralized database that works as a type of ledger for financial transactions. Due to the way it is secured, it is both easy for authorized users to access and very difficult for unauthorized users to access, for reasons that will be explained in detail in the later chapters. As the name implies, a blockchain is made up of individual blocks that each contains unique transaction information as well as information relating to his or her unique place in the chain. Every time a new block is added to a blockchain from an authorized node, that information is then shared with all the other nodes that make up the network after it has been verified. No centralized authority needs to tell the nodes to seek new information.

The earliest versions of what would go on to be blockchain technology was created in the 1980s by a programmer who was looking for a wait to stop spam email from clogging up his inbox. The impetus for what would eventually become blockchain technology is a proof of work model which is essentially a math problem that gets harder and harder, the more times it is called upon to verify details at once. As such, solving the equation to send a single email was something that 1980s computers could handle, solving it 10,000 times to send out a spam email was not. This same proof of work model is used in modern blockchain technology and explains why individual transactions need to be verified.

After its creation, the proof of work model only saw limited use until 2008 where it started gaining traction as a hypothetical means of facilitating a digital type of currency that wouldn't be bound by the traditional financial framework in an online peer-to-peer forum. While it was just a talk at this point, one of the members of the discussion, someone or a group of people using the alias Satoshi Nakamoto, took the conversation more serious than the rest and went to work creating the original design document for blockchain technology, and bitcoin as well, called bitcoin: A P2P Electronic Cash System, along with the code that would become the basis of the modern bitcoin blockchain. With proof of their ideas in hand, many new programmers jumped on the blockchain bandwagon, and soon the Nakamoto alias was never heard again.

When it comes to security, the blockchain does not take any offensive measures against threats and instead relies on extreme defense to win the day. As transactions need to be verified before they are added to the primary blockchain, any malicious blocks that may be sent will be automatically picked up and discarded before they can infect the whole block-chain. Only when all of its data lines up with at least 51 percent of all other nodes, a new block will be added to the blockchain. While, technically, it is possible to generate enough fabricated cloud to add a fake block to a chain, the resources required to do so are beyond the means of modern hackers and the costs for doing so would outstrip the gains.

In addition to storing information, the block-chain automatically timestamps the data which means it is extremely easy to determine when a given transaction took place after the fact. When all of its facets are taken together, it becomes easy to see why blockchains can essentially act autonomously with new blocks being created and assigned, and the whole being policed for errors, without anyone actively stepping in and taking control over any of it.

How does the Blockchain technology work?

So, now that we have spent some time discussing blockchain and some of the benefits that come with this technology, it is time to understand how this type of technology is going to work.

Since we will mostly associate blockchain with Bitcoin and some of the other digital currencies that are out there, it is easiest to take a look at how blockchain will work on these networks. It will work similarly on other networks as well, but this will help to keep things in order. On the blockchain, when you complete a transaction, it will end up showing up, in order, on one of the blocks you are using. When the block is filled up, it will join in the permanent record and will link together with the other blocks that you have completed to form a chain. This all works together to help keep your information in order and keeps it secure from others who may want to take a look at the information.

Each block in the blockchain is going to be responsible for holding onto all the important information about the transactions that you've completed and each of the blocks will hold onto a lot of data. Depending on the network that you work with, these blocks could contain information about currencies, digital rights, identity, and property titles to name a few. Since these blocks can hold onto so much information and will keep that information safe, blockchain is one of the best ways to help people interact, send money, and even make their purchases.

When you decide to join the Bitcoin network, and you create your own Bitcoin address, you will join in on its blockchain. Each user will receive a block that they will be able to fill up each time they finish a new transaction. These blocks can hold onto quite a bit of information, and some people will fill them up quickly, and others may take a bit longer.

After the block has been filled up with the different transactions that you are working on, they are going to become a part of the permanent record on Bitcoin. They will join the Bitcoin network's blockchain, and you will start making your own personal blockchain which will just contain all of the blocks that contain your own transactions.

When one block is all filled up, it is time to receive another block, which the system will automatically send over to you. You can then start to fill up that block with transactions as well, and the process keeps going for as long as you keep using the network. Every user on the Bitcoin network, or whatever platform you are using at the time, will have their own blockchain that is full of personal transactions. But as the blocks fill up, those will be added to the permanent blockchain that the Bitcoin network relies on, so the information is kept safe. This process works together to make sure the Bitcoin network remains transparent to use.

This can all seem a little bit confusing right now, but one way to think about how blockchain works is to think of it as your own bank statement. Each block you receive will be like a monthly statement that you get from the bank. You can look over it to see what transactions you have completed in recent times and check to make sure it is all good. After you have finished a few of these statements, they will all become part of your bank history. They will be a part of your permanent record with the bank (or regarding the blockchain, with the Bitcoin network), and you can always look back to see what payments you have made, what funds you have received, and any other transaction. The main difference between them is that blockchain is going to be online and will only be in charge of things that happen on the Bitcoin network.

One nice thing that comes with the blockchain technology is that it works with Bitcoin to keep your transactions safe and secure. There are some special codes or some hashes that will be added in so that hackers and other people will not be able to steal your information. Anyone who is on the network can see these transactions, but they will have to look through these special hashes to see what is going on. It is the work of the miners on the Bitcoin network that will make sure the blockchain ledger is secure, and they will be rewarded with 25 Bitcoin each time that they are successful.

The job of the miner may sound easy, but some complications can come with it and they are in charge of maintaining most of the security of this system. They will need to come up with the unique hashes that will help to hide up all of your information so that it will be safe from others who want to look. But they cannot just go through and write out any random number that they would like, or anyone could do this, and all of the coins on Bitcoin would be mined.

Instead, there are a few rules to the hashes that are created. First, the beginning of each hash needs to have a certain number of zeroes, and since you do not know how a hash will look until you are done, you could create quite a few of these before getting the results. Also, the hashes have to be designed so that if any one character in the chain is changed, it is going to change up all of the characters that come after it as well. This makes it complicated to make a good hash, but it does make it easier to catch if someone has been messing around in the blockchain.

As you can guess, the process of creating one of these codes is not the easiest, but these rules ensure that your information is going to stay safe and not just anyone could add in a random code to the mix. If they could do that, then a code could do the work, and the security would be gone. Right now, the miners will be rewarded with 25 Bitcoin when they are done. Since Bitcoin is worth about $3200 right now, this can be a good reward for the work they are doing. This becomes a win-win situation for everyone who is involved. The miners will get paid well for the work that they are doing, and the users of the network can rest assured that their information will stay safe.

The blockchain is a really neat piece of technology that has so many potential applications for users to enjoy. Right now, it is the leading force that has helped Bitcoin become so popular, but it is sure to change many other aspects of our world in the future. It is such a simple idea, just a ledger to keep track of transactions, but it is so efficient and easy to use that many platforms for different applications are already in use.

Chapter 5

BITCOIN MINING

What is Bitcoin Mining?

Simply put; Bitcoin mining is the process whereby new Bitcoins are generated. When fiat coins are minted, metal sheets are fed through a machine that presses out blank coins. Those coins are then impressed with a design that designates their value. Because Bitcoin does not exist as cash, new Bitcoins must be created through a different process. That process is mining. Bitcoin mining serves an additional purpose, as well: it is the process whereby transactions are verified and added to the public ledger.

The first Bitcoin block — the Genesis block — was mined by Satoshi Nakamoto on January 3, 2009. Since then, thousands upon thousands of blocks have been mined, leading to millions of Bitcoins being in circulation. There is an upper limit to how many Bitcoins can be in circulation; only 21 million can be produced, and that cap is expected to be reached in about the year 2140.

How Bitcoin Mining Works

To work properly, the Bitcoin network needs a lot of people. If only a handful of people were operating the network, those few people could collude together to manipulate all of the data in the blockchain and make themselves rich. Bitcoin would quickly become an oligarchy rather than a peer-to-peer currency.

Additionally, it would functionally revert back to the client-server model that is prone to hacking and security breaches, the very thing that blockchain was created to prevent.

The diagram below illustrates the difference between the traditional client-server model and the peer-to-peer network that Bitcoin uses.

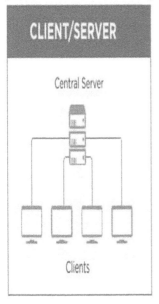

CLIENT/SERVER

Central Server

Clients

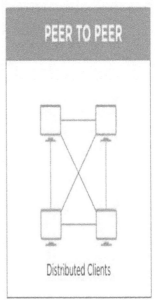

PEER TO PEER

Distributed Clients

In the first picture, you see that all of the computers must connect to a central server to receive their information. What happens if the server is somehow corrupted (say that it contains a virus or has been hacked so that all of the information in it is being siphoned off to someone)? Well, all of the computers connected to that server will fall prey, in some way, to whatever has occurred within the server.

Blockchains such as Bitcoin operate as a peer-to-peer network, as seen in the second picture. This means that instead of connecting to a central server, the users connect to each other.

While there may certainly be some unscrupulous individuals on the network who are trying to find weaknesses to exploit, their missions will fail unless they can convince every single other person on the network to join in on their shenanigans. It would take every single user on the network to override the verification process and retroactively manipulate any of the information contained in the blockchain's digital ledger.

Enter the process of mining, a built-in fail-safe mechanism that enhances the verification process. Users all over the globe connect their computers to the Bitcoin network, thereby actually contributing their computer's power and resources to upholding the blockchain. These computers store the entire blockchain on special software for the purpose of validating new transactions. The entire network must agree on new transactions that have occurred to prevent a problem known as double-spending. Double-spending is what happens when someone attempts to spend the same value twice. For example, imagine that Bob has $10 in his bank account, and he owes both Jim and Joe $10 each. Bob thinks of an easy solution: simultaneously write two checks, each for $10, and the bank will refuse to cash the one that is brought last.

With Bitcoin, there is no central bank to refuse the second check (or transaction), so how can the network ensure that no one spends a

Bitcoin value twice? When creating Bitcoin, Satoshi Nakamoto implemented a process called proof-of-work to ensure against double spending. Proof-of-work is, as the name implies, a process that ensures that work was done to carry out the transaction. Remember that all of the information contained within a block of transactions must be verified before it can become a part of the Bitcoin blockchain. The information is combined with the hash of the previous block to create a new hash, a cryptographic puzzle that must be solved for the block to be verified. If a shred of information within the block is changed, if so much as a comma is added or space is deleted, the entire hash will change. Things will get really messy for the rest of the blockchain because that hash value is used to generate the hash value of the next block. Everyone on the network will know that someone tried to tamper with that information, and the attempt to manipulate it will fail.

Miners, people whose computers are connected to the Bitcoin network to verify the transactions, use their computing power to solve the puzzle. Basically, their computers generate a series of random guesses. It takes about 10^{21} number of guesses to generate the correct answer, which equals a lot of computing power! It actually takes about 10 minutes for a computer to generate the answer, meaning that transactions take about 10 minutes to process. Some new computer chips and programs have

277

been generated, which increase the speed at which the computer can find the answer. More computing power means the ability to generate more of these random guesses, thereby increasing the probability that one of those guesses will be correct. Whoever comes up with the correct answer first wins a reward of new Bitcoins, which are generated through the process of verification. As technology evolves and miners are able to come up with the answer faster, the difficulty level of the algorithms increases. This is to ensure that a certain amount of work is still done to verify the transactions and that only a certain number of Bitcoins are in circulation.

Mining isn't free. It can be a great way for people to earn extra money, as long as their computers are incredibly efficient regarding power. For mining to be cost-effective, the cost of the energy used to power the computer must be less than the amount of money generated by the rewards. Let's go back for a minute to the idea of retroactively changing information in a block. Remember that if any information is changed, even just a measly period or apostrophe, the entire hash will change, which therefore changes the hash of every subsequent block in the blockchain. What this means is that you would have to go back and re-mine every single block! If mining one block takes 10 full minutes and a whole lot of computational power (read: money in the form of energy), then even if you could find a way to go back and retroactively change the information, the process would be cost-prohibitive.

So, how does this process of mining and verifying blocks prevent the problem of double spending? Consider that it takes about 10 minutes to verify a single block of transactions. A naive user might assume that he has 10 minutes to spend that amount as many times as he wants. Imagine that Emil has a total of one Bitcoin in his account. He buys a used car from Emily using that one Bitcoin. A split-second later, he uses that same Bitcoin to buy a riding lawnmower from Emilia. Each of those transactions will be sent to every single node on the network; given the sheer size of the network and latency involved, it is entirely feasible that the second transaction will get delivered before the first one and therefore be verified first. The other transaction will not be able to be verified, and unfortunately, Emily will have to find someone else to buy her clunker.

Chapter 6

BITCOIN WALLETS

What is a Bitcoin Wallet?

If you have cash, you probably store it in some type of wallet. Otherwise, your money just isn't safe. If you have ever seen someone walking around the mall with money inadvertently hanging out of his pocket, you are probably familiar with the urge to reach out and take it. Wallets are designed to keep your cash, and other confidential items like your credit and debit cards, safe. You probably store your wallet in a safe place and routinely check to make sure that everything that is supposed to be in there is, in fact, in there.

Now, your wallet can have everything in it that it is supposed to have and still be stolen. If an unscrupulous someone finds out where you keep it, or you happen to leave it laying around somewhere, it will be gone with little hope of ever recovering it. Hence, while the wallet itself exists to protect its contents, you as the owner of the wallet must take the steps to ensure that that wallet itself is safe.

Bitcoins need a wallet too. Since Bitcoins don't exist in cash form but are actually a part of a computer program, they can't be kept in the same kind of wallet that you hold your cash and credit cards in. There are special types of wallet that are designed to hold your Bitcoins. Bitcoin wallets are very similar to bank accounts. They display your current balance and any transactions that you have engaged in.

Bitcoin itself is more secure than the United States government websites. It is impregnable and immutable. However, security breaches have happened. These breaches aren't able to attack the actual Bitcoin code and software, but rather attack the wallets and exchanges that are used to hold individual users' Bitcoins. As you will see, while the wallets are designed to keep your Bitcoins safe, ultimately you are the one who is in charge of the wallet's security. Companies that host wallets must guarantee a certain level of security (otherwise, no one would use their wallets), but you must take measures on your own to ensure that your security is not compromised. This chapter will look at the different types of wallets available and help you make the best decision as to which wallet is right for you.

Hot wallets: All cryptocurrency wallets fall under two categories: hot and cold. A hot wallet is one that is connected to the internet and therefore can make faster transactions. Hot wallets are best suited for people who need to access their Bitcoin accounts fairly often to make a lot of transactions. Those who use Bitcoin to do a lot of trading may find that a hot wallet is the most beneficial for their needs. The downside of a hot wallet is that it is more vulnerable to hacking and other security breaches. Major Bitcoin hacks, such as the one at Mt. Gox, involved hot wallets.

Cold wallets: A cold wallet is one that is not necessarily connected to the internet and can be accessed and used without an internet connection. Transactions made with cold wallets can take considerably longer, so they are not suited for people who want to use Bitcoin for a lot of purchases. Because they are not connected to the internet, cold wallets are much more secure from security breaches.

Thin wallets: Thin wallets are a type of wallet that does not connect to the entire blockchain. Rather, it connects to a single node on the network, and from that node, the transactions are broadcast to the entire network. Thin wallets save a lot of time and storage space because the entire blockchain does not need to be downloaded.

Mobile wallets: A mobile wallet is one that is designed to work on an Android or iOS mobile platform. Mobile wallets allow you to take your Bitcoins with you anywhere you go, and some even allow you to make on-the-spot transactions, similar to Apple Pay. However, they are probably the least secure of any type of hot wallet. The private key is stored on the mobile device, so if the mobile device becomes compromised in any way, the private key could be exposed. This could lead to the entire Bitcoin account being compromised.

Hardware wallets: A hardware wallet is a type of cold wallet that exists as computer hardware. They include things like USB drives and smart cards. The private key is usually embedded within the hardware and therefore much less prone to being stolen. Regarding online security, hardware wallets are probably the most secure type of wallet. However, keeping the hardware itself secure is imperative. Hardware wallets can cost $100 or more, so they aren't for people who just want to experiment with Bitcoin.

Online web wallets: Online web wallets are a type of hot wallet that store all of the account information on the cloud. They are ideal for people who make a lot of online Bitcoin transactions. However, they are also the least secure.

Physical wallets: A physical wallet is a type of cold wallet that can be printed out and stored in a safety deposit box for an indefinite period of time.

Desktop wallets: A desktop wallet can be considered as a "warm wallet," as it is neither entirely hot nor cold. It exists as software downloaded to your computer desktop, which can be used when connected to the internet. Keep in mind that you should not store large amounts of Bitcoin on your desktop because if the desktop becomes compromised, so does your account.

Bitcoin clients: Bitcoin clients are the wallets originally used by the founders and are associated with the Bitcoin core. They are the opposite of thin wallets, as they are connected to the entire network and contain the entire blockchain.

How to Choose the Best Bitcoin Wallet for Yourself

To choose the best Bitcoin wallet for yourself, you need to know what are your own goals for using Bitcoin. If you want to use Bitcoin for everyday transactions — everything from buying coffee to buying things off of overstock.com — then you will probably want to use a hot wallet. Additionally, if you want to engage in trading, you will also want to use a hot wallet. Because a hot wallet is connected to the internet and can process transactions faster, it is best suited for people who want to make frequent transactions. If you want to use Bitcoin as a type of investment so that your money can grow in tandem with the exponential growth of Bitcoin's value, then you will probably want to use a cold wallet. Cold wallets are not adapted for frequent purchases but are great for storage. If you are concerned about security, then you will probably also want to use a cold wallet, as it is much less likely to be hacked.

How to Store and Secure Your Bitcoin Wallet

Securely storing your Bitcoin wallet is of the utmost importance. Besides choosing a reputable company to host your wallet, there are several different steps that you can take to maintain the integrity of your wallet and Bitcoin account. The most important thing is to never, ever, ever share your account information. Your private key is what the blockchain uses to process transactions from your account; if it becomes compromised, some unscrupulous individual will be able to go in and drain out your entire account.

Another thing that you can do to maintain your wallet's integrity is to use several different wallets, especially if you have a large amount of Bitcoins.

That way, if one wallet becomes compromised, the rest of your money will still be intact. Avoid reusing addresses to send and receive Bitcoin, and make sure to create multiple secure backups of your wallets.

Chapter 7

THE BITCOIN CORE

What is the Bitcoin Core?

The Bitcoin Core is the software that upholds the Bitcoin network. It was originally released by Satoshi Nakamoto in 2009 under the name Bitcoin. It was updated and renamed Bitcoin-Qt, and now is referred to simply as the Bitcoin Core.

Because transactions are constantly being made and verified as the data passes to all of the computers in the network, there are always several different versions of the blockchain. The purpose of the Bitcoin Core is to determine which version of the blockchain is valid.

The Bitcoin Core does not exist on a single server but rather is downloaded to the node computers that uphold the network. This feature helps ensure the ongoing decentralization feature of Bitcoin. Those who operate the Bitcoin Core receive special privileges, such as a higher level of security for their Bitcoins and a wallet that contains better privacy features.

Getting Started with the Bitcoin Core

If you want to get started with the Bitcoin network by becoming a part of its core, the first thing you need to do is go to https://Bitcoin.org/en/Bitcoin-core/ to download the core. Make sure that you go exactly to that address instead of doing a Google search, as there are counterfeit versions of the core that are actually malicious wallets designed to steal your Bitcoins. As of the summer of 2017, the total size of the entire blockchain is 130GB, so you will need to have enough free space on your computer to download it. You will also need to make sure that your computer is completely free of viruses and other infections.

Depending on the speed of your computer, downloading the blockchain can take anywhere from a few hours to a few weeks. Make sure that your computer is connected to a power supply and stays on so that the downloading process won't be interrupted. Once it is fully downloaded, you will need to set up the wallet connected to it by clicking on "Settings," then "Encrypt wallet." Enter in a unique password that you will remember; if you forget the password, you will not be able to reset it. The Bitcoins in your wallet will be lost forever. Once you set up the wallet, your computer will automatically shut down. Restart your computer and backup your wallet onto a USB drive that is used only for this purpose. Now, you are all set to use the Bitcoin Core.

The Bitcoin Source Code

Bitcoin is open source, meaning that anyone with programming knowledge can add to the source code. The source code is written in C++, so to work on it, you need to be knowledgeable in that programming language. You can go to GitHub to download the source code and create a pull request for changes that you wish to make. Those changes must be approved by an experienced programmer, so you may have to wait a while before your pull request is approved. Gavin Andersen, the current lead programmer, and developer for Bitcoin has suggested that programmers test out their code changes before submitting them for implementation. You can do so via TestNet.

Building Bitcoin Software from Source Code

Since Bitcoin is open source, you can contribute to the Bitcoin community by building software onto the source code. Maybe you have a great idea for how you will improve some aspect of Bitcoin or fix what you see as a problem.

Building software is a great way for technophiles to become a part of the Bitcoin movement.

How you build Bitcoin software from the source code will depend on what operating system you have. Ubuntu, Unix, Windows, and different versions of Mac OS will all have different starting points from which to build software. Nevertheless, the programming language used for Bitcoin is C++, so in order to build on it, you must be familiar with that language. C++ uses a lot of memory, so you will need an additional 1.5GB to 4GB of memory available before you can get started. There are many online tutorials available to help you get started with contributing to the Bitcoin community by building Bitcoin software from the source code with the particular operating system that you are using.

Chapter 8

THE PROS AND CONS OF BITCOIN

Being markedly different from traditional fiat currency, Bitcoin has various pros and cons. If you want to become a part of the Bitcoin movement and are still trying to weigh whether or not it's worth the money and effort, this chapter will help you decide if the pros and benefits outweigh the cons and risks.

Pros

Pro 1: It's decentralized: This book has already extensively outlined Bitcoin's decentralization. Because it runs on a peer-to-peer blockchain rather than through a centralized authority, Bitcoin cannot be manipulated in any way. No one or entity, not even Satoshi Nakamoto can implement any policy, change any information, or change the source code (only with approval) unilaterally. This means that Bitcoin works with a pure model of economic supply and demand, which makes it more viable than fiat currencies that are centralized.

In addition to not being able to be manipulated, the decentralization of Bitcoin means that it is trustless. What this means is that there are no middlemen or trusted third parties involved in any transaction. When you wish to pay for your groceries using your MasterCard, that purchase has to go through a third party, in this example, the MasterCard Company. You must trust that the company is taking its own internal measures to ensure that you are not charged twice for this one purchase and that it is behaving ethically, especially in regards to your account. If you take out a student loan through the United States government, you must trust that the third party — Sallie Mae — is engaging in ethical conduct, is not misappropriating funds, and has adequate security to prevent the system from being hacked; if it were not doing so, your account could be compromised. When you make a payment to your MasterCard or Sallie Mae account, you are trusting that the institution will apply the payment to your account correctly. Numerous companies — including Enron and Goldman Sachs — have fallen and people have lost trillions of dollars because of poor policies and management by trusted third parties.

Trustless means that you don't have to engage a trusted third party to complete a transaction. Because the information is broadcast to everyone on the blockchain and must be verified with a proof-of-work protocol, the network is fail-safe without the involvement of a third party. Since Bitcoin's inception at the beginning of 2009, no third party has had to come in to mediate any type of dispute. You may have to trust a third-party wallet, such as Kraken, but the blockchain itself does not require any trust.

The trustless feature of blockchain is so powerful that a programmer named Vitalik Buterin, who worked on Bitcoin software, saw its potential in creating something called smart contracts. A smart contract is an entirely digital, entirely enforceable contract held on a blockchain. An example would be if Emir is paying premiums to an insurance company for a health insurance policy through a smart contract. He develops pneumonia and must spend a week in the hospital. Instead of a claims adjuster or other type of negotiator trying to bring down the payments that the insurance company is responsible for, the smart contract automatically releases a certain amount of money to Emir to pay for his hospital stay. There are no angry phone calls, no hassling back and forth with demands that the insurance company pays what it owes, no hospital or insurance liaison trying to explain why only this certain amount was paid. Buterin used smart contracts to develop Ethereum, a blockchain network that developers can use to design their own apps. The potential of trustless smart contracts is virtually endless because they inhibit the potential for any corruption from either party involved.

Pro 2: It's easy to set up: Setting up a bank account or getting a new credit card can be an exhausting process. You have to either go to the bank or the credit card's website, wait in a long line, fill out a lot of information, call family members to find out some of the information, and hope that the bank or credit card approves your account. You have to hand over to the financial institution a lot of personal information, including your address, social security number, references, date of birth, place of employment, income, etc. It can be stressful knowing that if that company's security is breached, all of your personal information can be compromised.

Getting started with Bitcoin is very, very easy. To buy Bitcoins, all that you need to do is set up a wallet with an exchange. To set up a wallet, first decide which type is best for you: a hot or cold wallet? Once you make that decision, decide whether you want a mobile wallet, a desktop wallet, a hardware wallet, etc. Go to the wallet's homepage, download the wallet (if applicable) or order the hardware (if applicable), and create an account. You are now able to buy Bitcoins through the wallet's exchange service.

Pro 3: It's anonymous: In addition to being much, much easier to use than traditional financial institutions, Bitcoin is entirely anonymous. You don't have to use your real name in connection with your Bitcoin account; in fact, many blockchain security experts advise you not to. You do not have to give out any personal information, nothing that could somehow compromise your identity. In addition to the anonymous feature of Bitcoin, you can take additional steps to ensure that you remain anonymous on the network. Don't use a thin wallet, always use a VPN when on the Bitcoin network, use multiple addresses, and don't connect your bank account to your Bitcoin wallet.

Pro 4: It's completely transparent: Nobody expected Enron to fail, not even auditors or the IRS. By all measures, it seemed to be doing quite well and was not in any type of financial trouble. However, unethical internal accounting practices were being used, making it appear that there was money when there was not. The lack of transparency with the internal accounting led to people losing trillions of dollars when the company collapsed.

With Bitcoin, there is no need to worry about unethical practices because the entire network is completely transparent. All transactions, excluding none, are visible to every single person on the blockchain network. Anybody can log in to it and see exactly what is going on. There is no question that your money is safe from unethical practices.

In keeping with the decentralization philosophy behind the Bitcoin movement, any changes to Bitcoin protocol must go through a 51% consensus of the entire community. The team of core developers cannot implement any changes on their own because they want to ensure that the network remains entirely transparent.

Pro 5: Transaction fees are minuscule: Many credit card companies impose a transaction fee — usually around $3 — which is usually incurred by the merchants. Three dollars may not seem like much, but imagine that you use your card five times in one trip to the mall. That's $15, not including interest that goes straight to the credit card company! The transaction fee is there to make sure that the credit card company makes money, which it undoubtedly will. Those transaction fees add up for retailers and actually drive up the cost of goods. For example, you can expect to pay 10 cents less per gallon of gas if you don't use a credit card because there won't be a transaction fee.

In contrast to the high transaction fees associated with credit cards, Bitcoin's transaction fees are quite low. They are associated with the cost of mining and ensure that miners are fairly compensated for their work. If you want your transaction to be processed within the next block — within 10 minutes — you can expect to pay $1.35. If you want it processed in the next three blocks — within half an hour — you can expect to pay $1.12. If you want it processed within the next six blocks — within the next hour — you can expect to pay $0.45. Because the fee is paid by you and not by the merchant, the cost of goods is not driven up.

Pro 6: It's fast: Have you ever looked at your bank statement and realized that some transactions are missing? Maybe you made a deposit that has not yet appeared on your account or a major purchase that has not yet been processed. As a result, your account may look artificially low or high, and you are responsible for knowing how much money is actually in there as opposed to how much is shown on your account page.

Bitcoin transactions are processed in as little as 10 minutes, so there is much less waiting time to see transactions appear on your balance. If someone sends you Bitcoins, you can expect to see them in your account within 10 minutes to an hour, depending on the speed.

Pro 7: It's non-repudiable: One way that fraudsters make money is by contesting payments that they legitimately made for goods or services that they legitimately received to get that money back into their accounts. Fraud by some people means that the cost is incurred by everyone who uses the same financial institution. For example, imagine that David used his Discover card to buy a hot airplane ticket for a flight that leaves in two hours. Once he has arrived at his destination, he calls Discover to report a fraudulent transaction for an airplane ticket. Unless Discover can find a way to prove that the same person was not on that flight (a gargantuan task, considering David could always insist that the flight was taken by a relative who looks a lot like him), it will have to refund him the money. Interest payments and other fees associated with Discover card, paid by all the users are used to cover the cost of David's fraud.

With Bitcoin, there is no way to get that money back unless the recipient returns the transaction. If David used his Bitcoins to pay for that airline ticket, there is no central authority to which he can appeal to fraudulently request that the payment be returned to him. His only hope is that the airline itself will return the money, which is a very unlikely scenario. Because Bitcoin is non-repudiable, there is less chance for fraud to occur.

Cons

Con 1: Lack of awareness and understanding: One con of Bitcoin is simply that not many people are aware of it or understand what it is about. While many have heard the term "Bitcoin," they don't necessarily have any clue what the Bitcoin movement is or how the cryptocurrency operates. Mainstream economists and publications routinely try to discredit Bitcoin and point out different events as being the end of the Bitcoin experiment. While these predictions are always proved wrong, that information may not be what people see in mainstream media. This lack of public awareness and understanding also means that there are not many retailers that accept payment in Bitcoins. Some do, such as Subway, Overstock, and Microsoft, as well as many small businesses. However, compared to the number that accepts the dollar, the number is actually quite small.

Furthermore, some precious few laws are surrounding the use of Bitcoin, which, for the most part, is a good thing. Its inability to be regulated by a central government is one of the reasons many people choose to use it. But what if a legal case were to erupt which involves the use of Bitcoin? Could that be held up in a court of law? How would the law recognize Bitcoin, as an actual financial asset or as part of an imaginary market? Some major scandals, such as that of the Silk Road and ensuing fraud by Shaun Bridges — one of the FBI agents tasked with unmasking the Silk Road — showed that the legal system will not circumvent Bitcoin. However, there is still very little legal precedent for how any disputes involving Bitcoin would be handled.

Con 2: Risk and volatility: Money goes through cycles in which it is worth more and then worthless. All stocks and investments fluctuate; none exist on an entirely upward or downward trend. Historically, Bitcoin has seen more than its share of ups and downs in the market, and those ups and downs tend to be quite large, especially compared to traditional investments and fiat currencies. Bitcoin has been known to lose 75% of its value or more in just a single day! This volatility has kept many potential investors from using Bitcoin.

However, a simple analogy may demonstrate why Bitcoin experienced so much volatility. In the early days of Bitcoin, there weren't many users. As such, any event could have tremendous implications for the entire system. For example, August 2012 saw a sharp plummet in the value of Bitcoin that was simultaneous with the US government shutting down a Ponzi scheme operating under the name Bitcoin Savings and Trust. Imagine that a bowling ball is dropped into a small, kiddie swimming pool. That bowling ball will make a huge splash, generate waves, and cause a lot of the water to leave the pool. Why? Simply because there wasn't much water to begin with. The force of the bowling ball (in this case, major events that can affect the Bitcoin market) appears to be much greater when there is less water (in this case, fewer Bitcoin users) there to absorb the force of it. Now, imagine dropping that same bowling ball into an Olympic-sized swimming pool. It will certainly create a splash and some waves, and may cause some water to overlap the edges of the pool, but will not disrupt the entire system the way that it did with the kiddie pool. There is more water there to absorb the impact. There are now millions of users on the Bitcoin network and trillions of dollars' worth of Bitcoins in circulation. While external events will certainly continue to affect the market, they are no longer able to do so with the extremes that they once were able to.

Con 3: Still developing: Blockchain technology is still in its infancy, and the Bitcoin network is still developing. Programmers are adding to it constantly. The fact that it is still developing means that its legal status could be in question, should a problem arise?

Con 4: Uses a lot of energy: The original value of Bitcoin that was published by New Liberty Standard was not connected to its financial viability but rather to how much money was required to generate the energy to create one Bitcoin. That move may have been quite symbolic because the entire Bitcoin network uses a LOT of energy. Think of how many thousands of computers are required to process one single transaction. Estimates are that by the year 2020, Bitcoin will use as much energy as the entire nation of Denmark! One challenge that Bitcoin will have to face is how to decrease the amount of energy that the network uses while not compromising security; otherwise, Bitcoin will simply not be able to remain viable in the long term.

Chapter 9

HOW TO BUY, SELL, AND INVEST IN BITCOIN

What to Look for Before Buying or Investing in Bitcoin

Before you begin buying or investing in Bitcoin, there are several things that you need to be aware of. One is the current state of the virtual currency market. While virtual currencies are growing at a rate many times faster than traditional investments, they are still much more volatile. Look at what Bitcoin's current value is and where it is regarding how much it has increased or decreased. Now is always a good time to invest in Bitcoin, but there are certain times that are better than others. When people are afraid that their investments might lose value, they tend to sell them off, hoping to regain as much of their value as possible before losing it all. If Bitcoin is in a bit of a slump — say, its value has decreased by 10% over the past week — that is actually the best time to buy. When people are worried about the value of Bitcoin and are selling it, you can get it cheaply. Its value has recovered after every single slump, so if it has lost value over the past few days, you will be able to get more Bitcoins for the amount of dollars that you invest. The first part of the adage "buy fear, sell greed" definitely applies in this situation.

Many other virtual currencies have come onto the scene and exploded in value since the rise of Bitcoin. These so-called "alt currencies" include Ether (used to power the Ethereum network), LSK (used to power the Lisk network), dogecoin, and Litecoin. Their values have increased tremendously, and some cryptocurrency experts predict that the Ether may soon surpass Bitcoin in value. If you are serious about investing in Bitcoin, you may want to invest in some other cryptocurrencies as well. That way, your portfolio will be diversified and have more potential for growth. In the extremely unlikely event that Bitcoin should tumble, you won't lose all of your investments.

Another is your own goals for buying or investing in Bitcoin. Are you hoping to become an overnight millionaire? Do you like the principles behind the Bitcoin movement and want to become a part of that community? Do you want to save for retirement or buy a new car or home through the money accrued through Bitcoin? If you are hoping to get rich, you probably should look into Bitcoin trading as well as mining. Wanting to become a part of the Bitcoin movement and reaping the benefits of its increasing value as a side benefit is definitely a viable and worthy goal. However, using it to save for retirement is probably not the best idea. Its value will most likely continue to increase for the foreseeable future; however, you do not want to risk your retirement on the possibility of a crash. If you are willing to take that risk, make sure you diversify with multiple cryptocurrencies.

Only invest what you are willing to lose. Instead of investing your nest egg, a great way to get started with Bitcoin buying and investing is to use the extra money that you may receive. Your Christmas bonus at work, a surprise check in the mail, money from a garage sale, or extra cash gained by working a side gig are all great forms of income for Bitcoin investing. If you lose the money that you made mowing your next-door neighbor's lawn, the damage is not nearly as catastrophic as losing $100,000 from what would have been your retirement fund.

Where and How to Buy Bitcoin

To buy Bitcoins, all that you need is a private address, which is provided when you first get your Bitcoin wallet. There are multiple different exchanges that you can use to buy Bitcoins, all of which come with their own advantages and disadvantages. Coinbase is the world's largest Bitcoin broker and is available in about 33 countries. It has high liquidity, meaning that the company is solvent and not engaging in risky trading practices, and high buying limits, meaning that you can buy more Bitcoins through it than with many other exchanges. Its simple interface makes it probably the easiest of all exchanges for new Bitcoin users, and you can buy Bitcoins instantly using a credit card. It charges an exchange fee of 3.75%, which is in the low range of what other exchanges charge. However, the payment methods that it accepts are limited, and there is some question about whether Coinbase may actually track how users spend their Bitcoins. Anonymity on the Bitcoin network is more difficult with Coinbase, as it requires the disclosure of some personal information to buy Bitcoins.

CoinMama, based in Israel, is another large exchange. Its fees are higher than those of Coinbase, especially for people using a debit or credit card instead of a virtual currency to purchase Bitcoins. However, it is available in a larger number of countries, as well as some states in the US. Users can buy up to $150 worth of Bitcoins without uploading any personal information, making it more anonymous than Coinbase.

Local Bitcoin is a peer-to-peer exchange, so unlike other exchanges, it does not utilize a third party for users to buy Bitcoins. Users agree to meet in person at an agreed-upon time and place to exchange Bitcoins in person for a pre-determined price. It is the most anonymous, private, and secure of all Bitcoin exchanges because all of the transactions occur in-person directly between the users. No validating personal information is required. All payment forms that the person holding the

Bitcoins will accept are considered to be valid. In some countries that either have outlawed Bitcoin or that exchanges do not operate in, Local Bitcoin is the only way for people to obtain Bitcoins. However, users must constantly be on the lookout for scams, as some unscrupulous users may try to sell fake Bitcoins for cash.

CEX.IO is an exchange that charges low fees for credit card users. It is valid in many countries and states in the US, and Bitcoins purchased are usually available in a couple of days. Bitcoins can also be transferred to credit or debit cards, but for higher fees.

One thing to keep in mind about all Bitcoin exchanges is that while Bitcoins may have an actual exchange rate based on the currency as a whole, the exchange may use a much higher exchange rate. For example, say that the current value of one Bitcoin is $5000. The exchange may actually use a rate of $7000 or even higher. Be aware of this potentially higher exchange rate, as it will impact how many

Bitcoins you can buy with the dollars that you have.

How to Sell Bitcoin

Some users choose to sell their Bitcoins for many reasons. Maybe the exchange rate is so favorable that they have decided to cash out their Bitcoin holdings. Maybe they were investing in Bitcoin while saving for a specific purchase or event, such as a vacation, and are now ready to take that vacation. Whatever the reason, there are several different ways to sell Bitcoins. Selling Bitcoins is a bit more complicated than buying them, but it can certainly be done.

One way is through LocalBitcoins. LocalBitcoins facilitates the in-person exchange of Bitcoins by people who live geographically close to each other. You can advertise on LocalBitcoins that you have so many Bitcoins that you want to sell for a certain amount of money. When another user responds, you can arrange a time and place to meet in order to make the exchange.

Another way is to sell them to an exchange. Whereas with LocalBitcoins you sell them to an actual person, this method would involve selling them to the exchange. Some exchanges, such as BitStamp and Coinbase, allow you to sell them your Bitcoins. Keep in mind that the exchanges are looking to make a profit, so you may not get the entire value of what your Bitcoins are worth.

An indirect way of selling your Bitcoins would be to use them for your regular purchases or even for a large purchase. For example, say you have $8000 in Bitcoins and need a car. Luckily for you, there is a nearby car lot that accepts Bitcoins. You could use your Bitcoins instead of dollars to buy the car.

The best way to ensure that you can get the most for your Bitcoins is to explore all of your options. Look at multiple exchanges to see how much you would be able to get at each different one. Look at Local Bitcoin to see how much individual users near you are willing to pay. If you have friends or family members who want to get in on the Bitcoin movement or are already Bitcoin enthusiasts, let them know that you want to sell and see what they will offer. You will be able to find the best deal and hopefully get more money for your Bitcoins if you explore multiple different options.

Investing in Bitcoin

While many users join the Bitcoin movement because they like what it stands for and want to use Bitcoins instead of dollars, a growing number of users see the potential of investing in Bitcoin. Investing in Bitcoin can be a great way to increase the value of your assets. However, before you get started, you need to be aware of some market psychology so that you can stay ahead of it instead of letting it beat you.

The value of Bitcoin fluctuates. A lot. It is generally on an upward trend — and quite a steep upward trend — but it can still change the value by up to 20% or more in just one day. You need to be able to weather these ups and downs without feeling the need to pull out all of your holdings. To do so, you may want to tune out of any Bitcoin news. This may seem counterintuitive because if you are now a part of the Bitcoin community, you probably do want to keep up with what is going on. However, seeing that your investment may be losing value can be very stressful and compel you to sell, even if Bitcoin remains on a generally upward trend. Don't look at graphs and charts about Bitcoin's value every single day. Don't install a widget that alerts you whenever there is a change in your investment's value. Instead, put the money into Bitcoin, try to forget about it, and let it grow. Be like Kristoffer Koch. He invested $27 in Bitcoin in 2009 and completely forgot about them until the spring of 2013. By then, their value had exploded to nearly $900,000.

Buying and Holding: When should you buy Bitcoins, and when should you hold? The easy answer is that now is always a good time to buy Bitcoins. If you have some extra cash that you want to invest, now is a good time to do so. Tomorrow is also a good time to do so. Next week will probably be a good time to do so. There is never a bad time to buy Bitcoins. However, sometimes are better than others. If the price is in a temporary slump, buy then, you will be able to get more Bitcoins per dollar that you spend.

Holding Bitcoins is always a good idea unless you absolutely need to cash out or use them in some other way to meet unexpected expenses. In all likelihood, their value will grow, even if there are periods of slumps in their value. Some people, however, want to go all in and, instead of holding their Bitcoins, want to engage in Bitcoin trading.

Trading in Bitcoins: Bitcoin trading, like any other trading, is the process of buying and selling Bitcoins as the price rises and falls. Long-term traders study trends over extended amounts of time to buy and sell Bitcoin at the most opportune times. They may buy up as many Bitcoins as they can when the price drops and sell off when the price goes up to turn a profit. They tend to hold their Bitcoins for a long amount of time — months or even years — so that they increase in value.

Short-term Bitcoin traders are those that make multiple trades within a day or even an hour. They have to be glued to their computers and be able to make trades within milliseconds, as the value of Bitcoin rises and falls at multiple times throughout the day. When the value rises, they sell and when the value sinks, they buy. While many investors follow this philosophy, the trick to short-term trading is to make those decisions within minutes or even seconds. Experienced short-term traders capitalize on Bitcoin's volatility and can make thousands of dollars a week.

To get started with Bitcoin trading, you need to find an exchange that will allow you to do so. Decide if you want to do long-term or short-term trading and what your goals are, then find an exchange that will best help you meet those goals.

Investing in Bitcoin Mining: In addition to buying and holding and/or trading the currency, another way to invest in Bitcoin is through mining. You could always build your own mining rig and mine Bitcoins the traditional way, as described in a previous chapter. That does carry some cons and risks, including the fact that you will have to pay for mining equipment in the hopes of reaping a profit. The equipment may overheat, there will be a constant humming noise from all of the machines working, the equipment will only be profitable for a limited amount of time, electricity bills may be quite large, you will constantly have to ventilate the machines, and your home may become quite warm from all of the machines running around the clock.

An alternative to traditional mining is called cloud mining, also known as cloud hashing. In cloud mining, you don't have to have your own hardware and won't run up your electricity bill. Cloud mining is when multiple computers connect to a remote data center and combine their processing power to generate the hashes of data blocks.

There are three types of cloud mining. The first is hosted mining, in which users lease the hardware from a data center and run it in their homes or other private location. There is usually a contract involved, in which you agree to run the hardware for a certain amount of time in exchange for a certain amount of Bitcoins paid per hash generated. The benefit to hosted mining is that you don't have to buy your own equipment — which can be quite costly — and are not responsible for the depreciation that occurs naturally.

The second type of cloud mining is virtually hosted mining. In a virtual hosted mining, either the user creates, or the hosting company provides a virtual private server. A virtual private server is a type of virtual machine that connects to the internet with a particular operating system. Users then install the mining software (no need to mess with the hardware!) and use the power from the virtual private server to contribute to the mining pool.

The third type of cloud mining and the most popular is leased hashing power. Leased hashing power is almost like buying a temporary share in the cloud mining company. Users can either buy or sell hashing power. To buy hashing power, they pay a certain amount of money (usually in Bitcoins) to the company, usually a mining farm, almost like an investment that will yield returns. To sell hashing power, users generate a contract with the company in which they use their own computing power remotely in order to add to the farm's hashing power.

The biggest downside to cloud mining is that there are a lot of scams. In fact, most cloud mining schemes are scams. Before starting a contract with a cloud mining company, do thorough background research. Find out if the company is reputable by looking for reviews of people who have used that company for cloud mining. Find out where the company's physical location is. If you suspect that you may be getting into a scam, you probably are.

Chapter 10

HOW BITCOIN CAN AND WILL DISRUPT THE FINANCIAL SYSTEM

The Bitcoin is vastly different than any other monetary system, other than the alt currencies that the movement spawned, is a given. What is surprising to many experts is how vast the movement has become and how it is beginning to incite change in the traditional financial system. The very first time that Bitcoin was featured in a mainstream publication was in April 16, 2011, edition of *Time*. Journalist Jerry Brito wrote an article entitled "Online Cash Bitcoin Could Challenge Governments, Banks," almost as a harbinger of what Bitcoin may ultimately do.

Biopower

The traditional financial system that currently exists today took thousands of years to develop. It is the product of an evolution from a system of bartering to the use of gold as a universal currency to a centralized government-based coinage to banks offering paper notes that they guarantee, almost as loans against the bank. Banks, as they exist today, offer important things for individuals: a secure place to store their money, an easy way to conveniently access their money, and a means for their money to grow via investments and savings. People use banks so that they can reap one or more of these benefits.

For banks to provide these benefits, they must necessarily incur costs. They have to pay for the building that houses the bank, the salaries of tellers and other employees that provide the services necessary for running the bank, the IT specialists who maintain the online forums and websites for the bank, advertising and promotions to attract new customers, etc. These things all cost the bank money, lots of money. It generates this money by charging fees for its services. Banks offer loans to customers so that they can receive interest, via lines of credit, credit cards, mortgages, auto loans, small business loans, etc. They charge high overdraft fees — sometimes more than $40 — when customers spend money that they don't have in their checking accounts. Fees are assessed when bank customers use an ATM outside of the bank's network and when non-bank customers access one of the bank's ATMs. Merchants are charged when customers use the bank's credit cards. All of these fees add up, generating not only enough to cover overhead expenses — staff salaries, building upkeep and maintenance, etc. — but to create a lot of profit for the people who run the bank. What this actually looks like on the ground is someone who is unable to pay for groceries or gas for the week may incur a large overdraft fee, which goes to fund the second vacation home of the bank's CEO. The current financial system leads to the rich getting richer and the poor getting poorer.

The client-server model that many traditional financial institutions still use is not just how the banks run their online platforms. It is symbolic of how the bank funnels money to itself via the common people. Think about it like this. In the client-server model, individual users connect their computers to the main server to access the information to their accounts. That information theoretically belongs to the users, but in actuality, it belongs to the bank. If there is any kind of problem with the server, the entire system will fail. Similarly, if there is a problem with the centralized structure of the bank, the bank will fail, and all of the money in it could be lost, minus what is insured by the United States government. Say that unethical accounting practices have been occurring for years, similarly to what happened at Enron. All of the individual users who have been connecting their resources to the bank, trusting that the bank will manage them properly, will fall victim to the scheme.

Consider an impending financial crisis: the student loan bubble. College students and their parents have borrowed heavily from the United States government to fund the ever-increasing cost of college education. They do so with the belief that a college degree will provide graduates with the opportunity for a better, high-paying job than what would be available to a high-school graduate. While that scheme makes sense on a micro level, what has actually happened is that so many people have borrowed so much money that young graduates who are trying to get on their feet and start their own lives owe tens, even hundreds, of thousands of dollars to the government. In addition to the loan principal, they pay high-interest charges. Most student loans have an interest rate of about 6%, which is pretty low unless you consider that 6% is applied to loans that run into the hundreds of thousands of dollars. Many college graduates are barely able to even pay the interest on their loans and are not making any kind of dent into the principal. Because they are saddled with this heavy debt, they are unable to do things like save for a home, buy a car, or do other things that their parents were able to do at their age.

The 20th-century French philosopher Michel Foucault referred to this paradigm as biopower. Biopower exists when a government or other institution extends a seemingly friendly, helpful service to its citizens, such as when a bank or a government offers financial services — loans or a checking account — to common citizens. In doing so, the government or financial institution can exert a high degree of control over citizens. Consider how much of your personal information is available to your bank. If you were to default on a loan held by the bank, that default will be displayed on your credit report and keep you from being able to rent an apartment, buy a home, sometimes even get a job. You know that you must work long hours, sometimes at a job that you don't like, to keep from defaulting. You aren't able to use that money for things that you enjoy, like, say, a date night or a vacation, but rather must give it to the bank. The bank has thereby implemented a high degree of control over many aspects of your personal life. That control is biopower.

Peer-to-Peer Over Biopower

The peer-to-peer structure of Bitcoin and other alt currencies eliminates the paradigm of biopower. When a small group of people is in charge of the bank, they can control many aspects of their customers' lives. When a large group of people engages in peer-to-peer currency, such as Bitcoin, they can take control of their own financial lives and reclaim the freedom associated with it. Banks charge high fees and interest rates. Bitcoin's fees are incredibly low. Instead of going to pay for the CEO's second vacation home, they pay miners to process the transactions on the Bitcoin network. Banks are centralized and vulnerable to attacks that could compromise your finances as well as personal information. Bitcoin is decentralized and impervious to attacks; moreover, personal information is not required to join the network. You cannot owe money to Bitcoin. You may owe money to other users and choose to pay in Bitcoins, but you cannot owe money to the Bitcoin network.

Similarly, to how the client-server model is symbolic of how banks are run, the blockchain model is symbolic of how Bitcoin is run. Thousands of users connect to the network to keep it running. No one person or entity is running things behind the scene. Everybody has to agree on transactions that have occurred. The money cannot be manipulated in any way.

Ultimately, people vote with their wallets. They may be unable to change how things are done at the bank, but they can move their money to Bitcoin and other virtual currencies. The growth of virtual currencies has grown at such an exponential rate that banks have begun taking notice and are realizing that this is not just a passing trend. As more and more money is allocated to virtual currencies, banks will have to revise their practices to maintain customers.

Chapter 11

Top 5 Mistakes to Avoid While Trading Bitcoin

So, you're ready to get started with Bitcoin. That decision could be the best one that you have ever made regarding taking back your finances and empowering others to do the same. There are some common pitfalls that you will want to avoid, which this chapter will point out.

Using Your Exchange's Wallet to Store Your Bitcoins

Exchanges are great places to facilitate the purchase of Bitcoins. They help keep the movement strong and moving forward. However, they have their limitations. Remember that they are third parties who are facilitating the purchase of Bitcoins; in effect, they run very much like banks. When you have money stored in your bank account, you don't physically have that money present on your person in the form of cash. Rather, you are trusting that the bank has on hand the liquidity necessary for you to use that money to make purchases. If the bank is no longer solvent, the money may be listed as being in your account, but it does not actually exist in the bank's vaults.

This scenario is what happened with several Bitcoin exchanges that collapsed, such as the colossal failure of Mt. Gox. Millions of dollars' worth of Bitcoins were held by Mt. Gox; however, the company fell prey to an internal security breach that siphoned off 700,000 Bitcoins. When people who had accounts with Mt. Gox tried to access their Bitcoins, they simply weren't there. The company did not have the liquidity to redeem them.

When you have Bitcoins, you don't actually have them in your physical possession. Even if you store them on a hardware wallet, they exist in digital form. What you do have is your own private key. When you store your Bitcoins in an exchange's wallet, what you are actually doing is handing it your private key and trusting that the Bitcoins listed in your account balance are actually present. In effect, the online exchange is the wallet, and you are putting your Bitcoins into another person's (company's) wallet instead of your own.

Instead, you should look for a dedicated wallet, either online or offline, depending on what your needs and goals are. In a dedicated wallet, your Bitcoins actually exist inside the wallet that you hold with your private key.

Storing all Bitcoins at a Single Place Without Proper Security

Remember that when you use Bitcoin, despite the high security inherent in the blockchain technology, you are responsible for the security of the Bitcoins that you hold. If you store them all in one single place with one single private key, then you run the risk of that private key being compromised and you losing all of your Bitcoins. Additionally, if that one place was to fail somehow, you would lose all of your holdings.

Standard practice is to hold Bitcoins in multiple places with different addresses and keys. This ensures that even if one private key is compromised, there is not a risk to all of your Bitcoins being lost. Make sure that the multiple wallets are not connected to each other so that if one is compromised, the other ones are not at risk.

A good idea is to keep multiple wallets for different purposes. One wallet could be a cold wallet for your Bitcoins to grow in value over time. Another wallet could be a hot wallet for you to make frequent online transactions. Another wallet could be a mobile wallet that you can use to buy a cup of coffee or pay for a restaurant meal. Because mobile wallets are the riskiest, that one would need to have the smallest amount of Bitcoins.

Panicking About Price Change

The value of Bitcoin changes all the time and is really nothing to be concerned about. It has proven its viability through multiple highs and lows and has shown that it is not going anywhere but is rather on an upward trend. The value of your Bitcoins will change, and that's OK. The only time you should be concerned about a price change is if you tried to short the market but ended up losing a lot of someone else's money.

If you want to be extra safe about the ever-changing value of Bitcoin when you use it to make a lot of online purchases, click to approve the purchase when Bitcoin is on the uptake. Its value rises and falls all throughout the day, so you can potentially get your purchases for less if you complete the transaction when the value of Bitcoin is higher.

Frequently Changing from One Currency to Another

Bitcoin is not the only virtual currency that is growing quickly. Many other virtual currencies are on a fast upward trend as well. Some, such as the Ether, are actually growing at a rate faster than Bitcoin. Many exchanges allow you to exchange between Bitcoin and another virtual currency. Some naïve users take advantage of this feature because they think that in doing so, they can capitalize on a growth spurt of another virtual currency. For example, if Bitcoin is in a temporary slump and lost $10 in value within the past 24 hours, during which period the Ether grew by $15, users may think that trading their Bitcoins for Ether makes perfect sense. However, all virtual currencies are volatile by nature. The Ether could lose that extra value within the next 10 minutes, while Bitcoin could regain what it had lost and then some in an hour. Ultimately, the value of other virtual currencies is measured against the value of Bitcoin. If Bitcoin tumbles, other currencies will follow suit. What will ultimately happen is you will just lose a lot of money on exchange fees.

If you want to also invest in another virtual currency, by all means, do so. But be prepared to weather the ups and downs of both that currency and Bitcoin.

Not Training Yourself Enough or Listening to Media

Media coverage of Bitcoin has been both a blessing and a curse. The *Time* article published in April 2011 generated a surge of interest in Bitcoin that caused its value to increase dramatically over the ensuing months. It indicated that Bitcoin did have the potential to destabilize the current economic system. However, the media doesn't always get it right. *Forbes* and *Businessweek* are just two economic-based magazines that have routinely said that investing in Bitcoin is a terrible idea. Do a Google search for Bitcoin, and you will quickly see that mainstream economists and magazines routinely predict the failure of Bitcoin. And they have been proved wrong every single time.

Instead of listening to what others say, you need to arm yourself with correct information about Bitcoin. Look at data on charts and graphs. Study historical trends of Bitcoin. Use that information to come to your own conclusions about how you should move forward.

Chapter 12

REAL WORLD USE OF BITCOIN

Bitcoin is more than just a concept in which people exchange digital money that somehow gains value without existing in cash form. It can be used for real-world purchases, for everything from ordering pizza (the first commercial purchase that used Bitcoins) to buying cars and apartments. Its use is only limited by the number of merchants who accept it. Even if a particular merchant doesn't accept Bitcoins, you can use your Bitcoins to buy a gift card to use.

Online Purchases

There is a growing number of online retailers that accept Bitcoins as a form of payment. Microsoft and overstock.com are two major online retailers that accept Bitcoins. Others include Virgin Galactic (which includes retail stores and the airline), Word Press, Reddit, OkCupid, Expedia, Dell, Wikipedia, Whole Foods, the online newspaper *Bloomberg*, and some Etsy vendors. Some eBay merchants also accept Bitcoin. Many of these online retailers provide services rather than physical goods, but some, such as Dell and Whole Foods, do provide physical goods. The fact that Bitcoin can be exchanged for physical goods rather than just digital services shows that it does have real value outside of the Bitcoin community.

Physical Goods

A growing number of vendors are accepting Bitcoin payments for the physical goods that they sell. To find out if your preferred vendor accepts Bitcoin, look for a sign saying that Bitcoin is accepted. If you know of a local small business, either online or in a physical store, that you think should accept Bitcoin, talk to the owner. The philosophy behind Bitcoin is similar to many small businesses, and many owners will be happy to begin accepting Bitcoin in exchange for their goods. If enough people request it, large retailers like Amazon and Wal-Mart may even begin accepting Bitcoin for their goods. Think of what a boost that would be to the movement!

While waiting for retailers like BestBuy and Amazon to accept Bitcoins, there is a way to work around that limitation. Gyft is a website that allows you to purchase gift cards for many different merchants using Bitcoins. You can use your Bitcoins to purchase, say, a $100 gift card to Amazon and then use that gift card to buy what you wanted. Indirectly, you are using your Bitcoins on that purchase.

E-commerce

Sending money can be quite an expensive endeavor. After all, the third parties who are handling the money need to be able to pay for things like salaries and IT. Because no middleman is involved, Bitcoin is a much cheaper alternative to services such as PayPal and the Western Union. You can send money to anyone who has a Bitcoin account as long as you know that person's private key. The transaction will involve a small fee, which is used to pay the miners to verify the transaction. There may be an additional fee associated with the wallet that you use, but it will probably be much lower than what traditional money senders charge.

Physical Stores and Establishments

Subway was one of the first mainstream brick-and-mortar companies to begin accepting Bitcoins as a form of payment. Stores that do not exist online, or that do exist online but also have physical establishments, are accepting Bitcoin in greater numbers. To use your Bitcoins at one of these locations, you will need to download a mobile wallet. Keep in mind that mobile wallets are the least secure, so don't keep large amounts of Bitcoins in them.

Overseas Transactions

Exchanging fiat currency can be quite expensive. Anybody who has done much traveling will know that this is true. Many banks and money exchanges provide services in which they exchange dollars for other currencies, but usually with heavy fees attached and a lower exchange rate than what actually exists, meaning that you get far less in the other currency than what your money is actually worth.

Because Bitcoin does not exist as a national currency, it maintains the same value across international boundaries. One Bitcoin is worth just as much in the United States as it is in the United Kingdom. You can go to a Bitcoin ATM and redeem your Bitcoins for the same amount of currency as what they are actually worth.

Additionally, you can use your Bitcoins to buy from foreign merchants who accept Bitcoins without having to worry about currency exchange fees. If you are in the United States and wish to purchase something from a merchant in China, you may incur additional fees related to changing dollars to yen. But if you use Bitcoins, there will be no fees because the currency is not changed for another currency.

Chapter 13

THE FUTURE OF BITCOIN AND THE CHALLENGES IT FACES

While nothing about the future can be certain, Bitcoin's future does seem to be more certain than many other things. In all likelihood, it will continue its upward trend of unparalleled growth and will continue to fuel a movement of decentralization. Some predict that Bitcoin's value could hit $100,000 within the next few years; seeing as it has no sign of slowing down, that prediction could very well become a reality.

However, Bitcoin has many hurdles that it will have to overcome in order to continue to grow and remain viable. One involves the tremendous amount of energy that is required to keep the network running. If there are 10,000 Bitcoin nodes working to verify transactions, then consider how much energy is consumed. One Bitcoin transaction actually takes about as much energy as it required to power a home for an entire day. Many would be miners, and other node operators have had to decline to join the network in that capacity because it would cost too much money. If the cost of mining continues to increase, more people will be priced out of the operation and Bitcoin will ultimately no longer be viable. It is extremely energy inefficient, so much so that its energy consumption could eventually derail the entire network. One proposed solution is to change the protocols so that not all of the nodes are required to verify a transaction; however, this move could compromise the network's security and even open up the possibility of double spending. A more likely solution would be to offer incentives to nodes that use solar power or another renewable form of energy. Renewable energy is much cheaper than that generated from fossil fuels. Whereas fossil fuels require surveying, building rigs, paying drillers, transporting across long distances, and processing, renewable energy doesn't require much more than the start-up equipment. One small windmill could easily power a large mining farm without incurring costs beyond that of building the windmill. Solar panels can provide practically free energy to any location that has ample sunshine. Incentivizing these forms of energy could decrease Bitcoin's energy consumption and carbon footprint, thereby allowing it to remain viable.

Another challenge that Bitcoin will have to face is its legal status. The IRS has declared that it is an asset and will be taxed as such. However, much needs to be clarified, considering that users can send and receive it as currency. Some people receive their paychecks in Bitcoins. Does this mean that they will be subject to payroll taxes, and if so, how will the IRS configure the exchange between Bitcoins and dollars? Considering the high volatility of

Bitcoin's value against the dollar, this feat will not be an easy one. Its value changes by the minute, sometimes even by the second, so how will the IRS determine how much should be used for payroll taxes without recognizing it as a currency?

In addition to figuring out how tax laws should apply to Bitcoin is the question of how it should be upheld in a court of law. Individuals engaged in Bitcoin-related Ponzi schemes have been prosecuted for money laundering and fraud. However, anonymity frequently prevents these individuals from being identified and brought to court. The question of whether the courts will one day be able to require Bitcoin users to be somehow registered so that they are not anonymous but is a very real one. Additionally, the question of how Bitcoin itself would be viewed in a court of law is in question. If the IRS does not view Bitcoin as a currency, then if a dispute were to erupt involving Bitcoin, what would be the court's stance on how it should proceed? There is no precedent. To solve this problem, the team of Bitcoin developers will need to seek legal counsel about what Bitcoin's legal standing should be.

Another challenge is how Bitcoin will continue to prevent regulation, as efforts to regulate it seem to be increasing. New York State has passed a law requiring companies to acquire an expensive BitLicense in order to receive payments in Bitcoins. The cost of the Bit-

License is so high that some companies have had to stop receiving Bitcoin payments. In other places such as the UK, EU, and Japan, traditional banks like Barclays and even government-run businesses have begun accepting Bitcoin. While these moves appear to be an acceptance of the cryptocurrency, some are concerned that they are actually underhanded attempts to regulate Bitcoin. If governments begin to accept payments in Bitcoins, they could foreseeably begin enacting laws regulating it. How Bitcoin will continue to grow and not be subject to regulation is a serious question.

Is Bitcoin the Next Gold?

Remember that gold became ubiquitous as a universal standard in trading. Instead of bartering goods, gold could be used across boundaries in order to procure and sell goods. From this perspective, Bitcoin could very well be the next gold. It is not connected to any one national currency but instead accepted freely across international borders; it is a type of new universal standard that can be used in much the same way that gold was.

Gold does not derive its value from what governments say that it is worth but rather from what the people who use it say it is worth. Governments can assign it as a value, but this value is only arbitrary and is subject to market fluctuations based on supply and demand. In this sense, Bitcoin is again like gold. While a dollar figure may represent how much Bitcoin is actually worth, its real worth is determined by the people who use it. Any dollar-based figure is merely an arbitrary representation of how much an entity thinks it is worth. What people are willing to pay for it, rather than what an exchange posts about its current rate, determines how much it is worth.

Bitcoin is different than gold in one important way, and this does not have to do with the fact that gold is a physical asset while Bitcoin is a digital asset. Bitcoin has something called social capital. Social capital is the power that is derived from having some people adhering to a particular cause. Bitcoin is more than a currency; it is a movement of decentralization against big government and large financial institutions that have crippled and simultaneously taken over the market.

It is a people's movement of taking away the biopower that was gained through centralized institutions providing services at a cost and replacing it with community-based peer-to-peer networking. With this movement growing day by day, there is absolutely no indication that Bitcoin will lose steam.

It has already spawned a revolution in computer technology by implementing blockchain, as well as a number of technologies such as Ethereum and other blockchain networks.

Even if the dollar value of Bitcoin continues to fluctuate, its true value lies in the movement that it founded.

Conclusion

Thank you for making it through to the end of Bitcoin, let's hope it was informative and able to provide you with all of the tools you need to achieve your goals whatever it may be. Just because you have finished this book does not mean there is nothing left to learn on the topic, expanding your horizons is the only way to find the mastery you seek. As bitcoin and blockchain is still such a new technology, there is no telling when new potentially game-changing information is going to emerge which means keeping your ear to the ground is the only way to actually ensure that you are not caught off guard.

The next step is to start your blockchain account and start investing with Bitcoin.

Hopefully, your venture with Bitcoin will be successful. Always keep in mind that it will be difficult in the beginning, so don't get discouraged when things don't go as you want for it will, eventually. Be patient, work hard, keep faith in your ability, and use this book as your ultimate guide towards your success.

Finally, before you go, I'd like to say "thank you" for purchasing my book.

I know you could have picked from dozens of books on this topic, but you took a chance with my guide. So, big thanks for downloading this book and reading all the way to the end.

Now, I'd like to ask for a *small* favor. Could you please take a minute or two and leave a review for this book on Amazon? This feedback will help me continue to write the kind of books that will help you get results and I would really value your opinion.

And if you love it, then please let me know ☺

Thank you and good luck!

Additional Resources

www.michaelnielsen.org/ddi/how-the-bitcoin-protocol-actually-works/

www.zen.lk/2013/11/28/how-i-finally-understood-bitcoin/

www.quora.com/What-is-Bitcoin-and-how-does-it-work-Is-it-legal-Whos-behind-it

www.bitcoin.com/guides/how-to-get-started-with-bitcoin

www.guscost.com/2013/12/15/bitcoins-cash-and-gold/

www.imponderablethings.com/2013/07/how-bitcoin-works-under-hood.html

www.blockchain.info/pools

www.bitcoin.org/en/developer-documentation

www.github.com/bitcoin/bitcoin/search?utf8=%E2%9C%93&q=source+code&type=

www.bitcointechtalk.com/a-gentle-introduction-to-bitcoin-core-development-fdc95eaee6b8?gi=1e6a8948ed03

www.en.bitcoin.it/wiki/Category:Technical

ABOUT THE AUTHOR

Neil Hoffman is a young crypto millionaire, an ex-army, and an online entrepreneur. He is also a self-taught computer programmer who currently lives in Chicago. As a self-made man, he is now willing to share with the public all his learning and knowledge about blockchain technology, bitcoin, cryptocurrencies and forex trading in a collection of books.

As an early investor of Bitcoin, Neil believes bitcoin and cryptocurrencies will revolutionize the world within the next decade.

The luckiest event of his life was to meet his mentor in 2012. Thanks to his mentor he was soon able to understand the online business and especially about investing in bitcoin and other cryptocurrencies. He quickly climbed up the ladder proving all his skills and talent.

He made a fortune trading bitcoin and crypto-currencies, he loves trading cryptocurrencies and forex and he sees it as having a huge potential to make some serious income. It is not easy as some would make you believe, but if you keep it simple, control your money management, and be consistent, then he thinks there is no reason that you too shouldn't succeed in the world of cryptocurrency trading.

During his spare time, Neil loves to visit different places around the world, taking pictures
and he really loves spending time in the gym.

Want to know more? Then check out the different books Neil has published.

CPSIA information can be obtained
at www.ICGtesting.com
Printed in the USA
LVHW112124120322
713325LV00004B/122